T0357366

Wealth Building Essentials

by Eric Tyson, MBA
with Bob Carlson, Robert S. Griswold MSBA CRE CPM, and Margaret Atkins Munro EA, and Jim Schell

for
dummies®
A Wiley Brand

Wealth Building Essentials For Dummies®

Published by: **John Wiley & Sons, Inc.**, 111 River Street, Hoboken, NJ 07030-5774, www.wiley.com

Copyright © 2025 Eric Tyson & John Wiley & Sons, Inc. All rights reserved, including rights for text and data mining and training of artificial technologies or similar technologies.

Published simultaneously in Canada

For general information on our other products and services, please contact our Customer Care Department within the U.S. at 877-762-2974, outside the U.S. at 317-572-3993, or fax 317-572-4002. For technical support, please visit https://hub.wiley.com/community/support/dummies.

Wiley publishes in a variety of print and electronic formats and by print-on-demand. Some material included with standard print versions of this book may not be included in e-books or in print-on-demand. If this book refers to media that is not included in the version you purchased, you may download this material at http://booksupport.wiley.com. For more information about Wiley products, visit www.wiley.com.

Library of Congress Control Number: 2025932930

ISBN 978-1-394-32619-8 (pbk); ISBN 978-1-394-32621-1 (ePDF); ISBN 978-1-394-32620-4 (epub)

SKY10099226_030325

Table of Contents

Introduction

Welcome to *Wealth Building Essentials For Dummies*. This book draws on my decades of experience working in the financial services industry as a financial counselor and bestselling author to help you create a plan to boost your wealth.

I know from working with people of modest and immodest economic means that they increase their wealth by doing the following:

>> Living within their means and systematically saving and investing money, ideally in a tax-favored manner

>> Buying and holding a globally diversified portfolio of stocks

>> Building their own small business

>> Investing in real estate

This book explains the essentials of each of these wealth boosters. You learn how to build a mindset toward wealth, pick smart investments, pursue revenue-building opportunities, and mitigate risk. And I help you keep wealth in its proper and balanced perspective.

About This Book

This book covers the essential financial strategies you can use to build wealth. I begin by helping you consider what wealth means to you in terms of boosting your assets and beyond. I also discuss the mindset required to be a successful wealth-builder. The chapters that follow discuss financial strategies you can use to boost your assets.

You can read this book from cover to cover if you want, or you can read a particular chapter or part without having to read what comes before it. Handy cross-references direct you to other places in the book for more details on a specific subject.

Foolish Assumptions

Every book is written with a certain reader in mind, and this book is no different. Here are some assumptions I made about you:

>> You may have some investment knowledge and investments, but you're looking to get serious about building and protecting long-term wealth.

>> You want to evaluate your investment advisor's or broker's advice or other investment ideas.

>> You have a company-sponsored investment plan, like a 401(k), and you're looking to make some decisions or roll it over into a new plan.

If one or more of these descriptions sound familiar, you've come to the right place.

Icons Used in This Book

The icons in this book help you find particular kinds of information that may be useful to you.

TIP

This icon denotes strategies that can enable you to build wealth faster and leap over tall obstacles in a single bound.

REMEMBER

I think the name says it all, but this icon indicates something really, really important — don't you forget it!

WARNING

With this information, I try to direct you away from blunders and mistakes that others have made when making important personal finance and related decisions.

Where to Go from Here

If you have the time and desire, I encourage you to read this book in its entirety. It provides you with the essential information you need to maximize return on your wealth-building efforts while reducing risk. You also can pick and choose the information you read based on your individual needs. Just scan the table of contents or index for the topics that interest you the most.

Chapter **1**

Developing a Wealth Mindset

I n this chapter, I encourage you to consider what wealth means to you. I explain how to think in terms of abundance, which is essential to cultivating a healthy wealth mindset. I also help you recognize the common flaws in mindset that lead to counterproductive financial habits, such as over-saving and accumulating too much debt. Think of this chapter as a touchstone you can revisit as you define your financial goals.

Focusing on Abundance

Wealthy people with a healthy and balanced perspective on wealth and life possess a mindset that focuses on abundance. They use and enjoy their money, and although this may sound counterintuitive, they resist over-saving.

Yes, it's true: Over-saving is possible. Some people, in fact often the best savers, get hooked on amassing more and more money and have trouble enjoying and using their money. Super savers and money amassers generally equate more money with more financial security. Theirs is a scarcity mindset.

This section can help you recognize this scarcity mindset in yourself and others, and provides tips to address and temper it.

Avoiding a scarcity mindset

Over-savers possess a scarcity mindset. Just as some people think that their financial problems would be solved if only they could earn a higher income, over-savers typically believe that if they could reach a greater level of assets, they'd be more relaxed and could do what they really want with their lives. The bar, however, continually gets raised, and the level of "enough" is rarely attained. For this reason, some of the best savers and money accumulators also have the most difficulty spending money, even in retirement.

Some super savers have insecurities relating to money. Specifically, they view amassing financial assets as providing them with safety and security that extend far beyond the financial realm. While having more financial assets, in theory, provides greater financial peace of mind, these riches don't necessarily provide more of the other types of security — friendships, for example, for which hoarders are searching.

Achieving a certain level of affluence can provide for greater access to quality healthcare. However, once one reaches the point at which quality healthcare is the norm, the incessant pursuit of more money can have a negative impact on an individual's long-term health and quality of life. For example, super savers often believe that they will be better protected as seniors and better able to enjoy their retirement years with hefty account balances. But the pursuit of more money, which typically entails longer work hours and greater stress, can lead to more health problems before and in retirement.

Many super savers, who also tend to be obsessed with work, come from homes and families where they felt on the edge economically and emotionally. Although there are so many things that we can't control in the world, money amassers typically derive a sense of both economic and emotional security from saving a lot of money.

Super savers have an amazing ability to selectively hear particular stories that reinforce rather than question their tendencies and beliefs. For example, stories periodically surface about how the legions of baby boomers retiring will bankrupt Social Security and cause a stock market collapse. Super savers batten down the hatches, save more, and invest even more conservatively when such stories worry them. News stories about stock market declines, corporate layoffs, budget deficits, terrorism risks, rising energy prices, and conflicts in the Middle East and elsewhere cause super savers to close their wallets, clutch their investments, and worry and save more.

Balancing spending and saving

Most people don't want to work their entire adulthood. And, even if they do enjoy working for pay that much, who wants to live on the edge economically, always dependent upon the next paycheck to be able to pay the monthly bills?

That's why you should avoid the extremes of overspending and over-saving. Consider the analogy to eating food: Eat too little or not enough of the right kinds of foods, and you go hungry and possibly suffer deficiencies of energy and nutrition; too much eating, on the other hand, leads to obesity and other health problems.

Overspending and its companion, under-saving, hamper your ability to accomplish future personal and financial goals and in the worst cases, can lead to bankruptcy. Over-saving can lead to not living in the moment and constantly postponing for tomorrows that we may not live to enjoy.

Remember Goldilocks and her quest at the bear's home for the bowl of porridge that was not too hot and not too cold and a bed to rest in that was not too hard and not too soft. Everyone should save money as a cushion and to accomplish important personal and financial goals.

> **>> Keeping money accumulation in proper perspective:** As with any good habit, you can get too much of a good thing. Washing your hands and maintaining proper hygiene is worthwhile, but it becomes problematic when you obsess over cleanliness and it interferes with your life and personal relationships.
>
> Conquering over-saving and an obsession with money typically requires a mix of education and specific incremental behavioral changes. Substantive change typically comes over months and years, not days and weeks.

The vast majority of super savers work many hours and may neglect their loved ones and themselves. They typically need to work less and lead more balanced lives. That may involve changing jobs or careers or simply coming up with a "stop-doing list," the opposite of a "to-do list."

>> **Giving yourself permission to spend more:** Money amassers usually need to discover how to loosen the purse strings. Figuring out how to spend more and save less is a problem more folks wish they had, so consider yourself lucky in that regard! Give yourself permission to spend knowing that the money you've saved will continue to grow and be available to you as you need it.

>> **Doing some retirement analysis:** Understand the standard of living that can be provided by the assets you've already accumulated. There are numerous useful retirement planning analytic tools you can use to assess where you currently stand in terms of saving for retirement.

TIP

Among the various mass market website retirement tools, I really like T. Rowe Price's (www.troweprice.com/usis/advice/tools/retirement-income-calculator) and Vanguard's (investor.vanguard.com/calculator-tools/retirement-income-calculator/).

>> **Getting smart about investing your money:** While super savers love watching their money grow, some have trouble with investing in volatile wealth-building investments like stocks because they generally abhor losing money. Even bonds can be a turn-off because they, too, can fluctuate in value.

So, part of the challenge with getting comfortable with spending more of your money is to get wiser about investing. Please see Chapter 3.

>> **Going on a news diet:** Super savers often benefit from minimizing and even avoiding news programs that dwell on the negative, which only reinforces your fears about never having enough money. One justification that super savers use for their actions that constantly resurfaces in the news is the litany of fears surrounding the tens of millions of baby boomers hitting retirement age around the same time. The story goes that retiring boomers will cause a mammoth collapse of the stock market as they sell out to finance their golden years. Real estate prices are supposed to plummet as

well, as everyone sells their larger homes and retires to small condominiums in the Sun Belt.

Such doomsaying about the future of financial and real estate markets is unfounded. The fear that boomers will suddenly sell everything when they hit retirement is bogus. Nobody sells off their entire nest egg the day after they stop working; retirement can last up to 30+ years, and assets are depleted quite gradually. On top of that, boomers vary in age by up to 16 years and, thus will be retiring at different times. The wealthiest (who hold the bulk of real estate and stocks) won't even sell most of their holdings but will, like the wealthy of previous generations, pass on many of their assets.

>> **Treating yourself to something special:** Regularly buy something that you historically have viewed as frivolous but which you can truly afford. Once a week or once a month, treat yourself!

By all means, spend the money on something that brings you the most joy, whether it's eating out occasionally at a pricey restaurant or taking an extra vacation during the year. How about tickets to your favorite sporting events or other performances?

>> **Buying more gifts for the people you love:** Money hoarders actually tend to be more generous with loved ones than they are with themselves. However, over-savers still tend to squelch their desires to buy gifts or help out those they care about.

Think about those you care most about and what would bring joy to their lives. Try hard to think about what they really value and enjoy.

>> **Going easy when it comes to everyday expenses:** How would you like it if a family member or close friend followed you around all day and totaled up the number of calories that you consumed? Well, then, why would you expect your family to happily accept your daily, weekly, and monthly tracking of their expenditures? In some families, super savers who habitually track their spending drive others crazy with their perpetual money monitoring. Personal finances become a constant source of unnecessary stress and anxiety.

Especially if you're automatically saving money from each paycheck or saving on a monthly basis, does it really matter where the rest of it goes? (Of course, none of us wants family members to engage in illegal or harmful behaviors. But other than that, enjoy life.)

Work at establishing guidelines and a culture of spending money that everyone can agree and live with. Some couples, for example, only discuss larger purchases, which are defined as exceeding a certain dollar limit such as $100 or $200. Parents who teach their children about spending wisely pass along far more valuable financial lessons than do elders who nag and complain about specific purchases.

Remembering that wealth is about more than numbers

REMEMBER

Getting bogged down in the climb up the career ladder, burning the midnight oil, and accumulating wealth and possessions is easy in a capitalist society. In your pursuit, losing sight of some areas — the ones not about money — is also easy. These areas are just as important as — if not more important than — your finances, which is why you should be working just as hard at planning them. Here are some ideas to get you started:

>> **Personal connections:** A lot of research shows that those individuals who have strong and healthy connections in their later years tend to be happier, enjoy better health, live longer, and live longer independently. Make sure you spend time making and maintaining healthy personal relationships. Doing so is an investment that pays dividends by improving the length and quality of your life.

>> **Personal health:** Your health is much, much more important than your financial net worth. Just ask folks who have major medical problems — especially those they could have avoided — if they wish they had taken better care of their health. Although anyone can experience bad luck or bad genes when it comes to health, you can do a lot to stay healthy and enjoy enhanced longevity and the best possible quality of life.

TIP

>> **Activities, hobbies, and interests:** Consider taking up activities and hobbies, part-time work, and volunteering. Giving something back to society pays many dividends.

You can find a zillion volunteer opportunities. Your place of worship, organizations that support a cause you believe in (for example, fighting cancer or heart disease), and schools are super places to start looking. Stumped for ideas? Try a service like VolunteerMatch (www.volunteermatch.org).

Developing a Wealth Mindset Toward Debt

Consider why you borrow money. Usually, you borrow money because you don't have enough to buy something you want or need — like a college education. A four-year college education can easily cost $100,000, $150,000, $200,000, $250,000, or more. Most people don't have that kind of spare cash. So borrowing money to finance part of that cost enables you to buy the education.

How about a new car? A trip to your friendly local car dealer shows you that a new set of wheels will set you back $25,000+. Although more people may have the money to pay for that than, say, the college education, what if you don't? Should you finance the car the way you finance the education?

There's a *big* difference between borrowing for something that represents a long-term investment and borrowing for short-term consumption. I'm not saying that you shouldn't buy a car. The point is to *spend what you can afford*. If you have to borrow money in the form of an outstanding balance on your credit card for many months in order to buy a car (or take the vacation, or whatever), then you *can't afford* it.

Avoiding bad debt

I coined the term *bad debt* to refer to debt incurred for consumption, because such debt is harmful to your long-term financial health.

You'll be able to take many more vacations during your lifetime if you save the cash in advance. If you get into the habit of borrowing and paying all the associated interest for vacations, cars, clothing, and other consumer items, you'll spend more of your future income paying back the debt and interest, leaving you with less money for your other goals.

The relatively high interest rates that banks and other lenders charge for bad (consumer) debt is one of the reasons you're less able to save money when using such debt. Not only does money borrowed through credit cards, auto loans, and other types of consumer loans carry a relatively high interest rate, but it also isn't tax-deductible.

I'm not saying that you should never borrow money and that all debt is bad. Good debt, such as that used to buy real estate and small businesses, is generally available at lower interest rates than bad debt and is usually tax-deductible. If well managed, these investments may also increase in value. Borrowing to pay for educational expenses can also make sense. Education is generally a good long-term investment because it can increase your earning potential. And student loan interest is tax-deductible, subject to certain limitations. Taking out good debt, however, should be done in proper moderation and for acquiring quality assets. See the section later in this chapter, "Assessing good debt: Can you get too much?"

REMEMBER

Borrow money only for investments (good debt) — for purchasing things that retain and hopefully increase in value over the long term, such as an education, real estate, or your own business. Don't borrow money for consumption (bad debt) — for spending on things that decrease in value and eventually become financially worthless, such as cars, clothing, vacations, and so on.

Assessing good debt: Can you get too much?

As with good food, you can get too much of a good thing, including good debt! When you incur debt for investment purposes — to buy real estate, for small business, even your education — you hope to see a positive return on your invested dollars.

But some real-estate investments don't work out. Some small businesses crash and burn, and some educational degrees and programs don't help in the way that students hope they will.

There's no magic formula for determining when you have too much "good debt." In extreme cases, I've seen entrepreneurs, for example, borrow up to their eyeballs to get a business off the ground. Sometimes this works, and they end up financially rewarded, but in most cases, extreme borrowing doesn't pan out.

Here are three important questions to ponder and discuss with your loved ones about the seemingly "good debt" you're taking on:

>> Are you and your loved ones able to sleep well at night and function well during the day, free from great worry about how you're going to meet next month's expenses?

>> Are the likely rewards worth the risk that the borrowing entails?

>> Are you and your loved ones financially able to save what you'd like to work toward your goals?

If you answer "no" to these questions, consider focusing on some debt-reduction strategies, such as those I cover in my *Personal Finance For Dummies* book.

Kicking a credit card habit

TIP

Here are some tips that can help limit the influence credit cards hold over your life:

>> **Reduce your credit limit.** If you choose not to take my advice and get rid of all your credit cards or get a debit card, be sure to keep a lid on your credit card's *credit limit* (the maximum balance allowed on your card). You don't have to accept the increase just because your bank keeps raising your credit limit to reward you for being such a profitable customer. Call your credit card service's toll-free phone number and lower your credit limit to a level you're comfortable with.

>> **Replace your credit card with a charge card.** A *charge card* (such as the American Express Card) requires you to pay your balance in full each billing period. You have no credit line or interest charges. Of course, spending more than you can afford to pay when the bill comes due is possible. But you'll be much less likely to overspend if you know you have to pay in full monthly.

>> **Never buy anything on credit that depreciates in value.** Meals out, cars, clothing, and shoes all depreciate in value. Don't buy these things on credit. Borrow money only for sound investments — education that advances your career prospects, real estate, or your own business, for example.

>> **Think in terms of total cost.** Everything sounds cheaper in terms of monthly payments — that's how salespeople entice you into buying things you can't afford. Take a calculator along, if necessary, to tally up the sticker price, interest charges, and upkeep of a car you may be considering, for example. The total cost will scare you. *It should.*

>> **Stop the junk mail avalanche.** Look at your daily mail — I bet half of it is solicitations and mail-order catalogs. You can save some trees and some time sorting junk mail by removing yourself from most mailing lists. To remove your name from mailing lists, contact the Direct Marketing Association (you can register through its website at www. dmachoice.org/register.php.) They now charge a $6 administrative fee for a ten-year registration period.

To remove your name from the major credit-reporting agency lists that are used by credit-card solicitation companies, call 888-567-8688 or visit www.optoutprescreen.com online. Also, tell any credit card companies you keep cards with that you want your account marked to indicate that you don't want any of your personal information shared with telemarketing firms.

>> **Limit what you can spend.** Go shopping with a small amount of cash and no plastic or checks. That way, you can spend only what little cash you have with you!

Chapter **2**
Practicing Mindful Spending

When you begin thinking in terms of building wealth, you question all the things you spend your money on to prioritize what's most important and reduce spending on those items that are not.

In this chapter, I encourage you to consider your spending habits. Is a second car more or less important than a vacation abroad? Are you willing to give up regular clothing purchases, or would you rather quit your gym membership and start exercising in other ways? And what about those new smartphones you've been buying for $600, $800, or perhaps even more?

I also describe the traits of successful savers and highlight the benefits of budgeting.

Keeping Lifestyle Inflation in Check

For most people, spending money is a whole lot easier and more fun than earning it. Far be it from me to tell you to stop having fun and turn into a penny-pinching, stay-at-home miser.

Of course, you can spend money. But there's a world of difference between spending money carelessly and spending money *wisely*.

If you spend too much and spend unwisely, you put pressure on your income and your future need to continue working. Savings dwindle, debts may accumulate, and you can't achieve your financial (and perhaps personal) goals.

Thinking like a saver

Here are the common traits among those who are able to consistently save a healthy portion of their income. Successful savers

>> **Understand needs versus wants.** Don't define necessities by what those around you have. I'm not going to tell anyone exactly how they should spend their money. But I will tell you that if you take out an auto loan to buy a car that you really can't afford, and you take a similar approach with other consumer items you don't truly need, you're going to have great difficulty saving money and accomplishing your goals and will probably feel stressed.

>> **Routinely question spending and value research.** Prior to going shopping for necessities that aren't everyday purchases, make a list of the items you're looking for and do some research first. (Consumer Reports is a useful resource.) After you're sure that you want an item; your research has helped you identify brands, models, and so on that are good values; and you've checked in with your bank or money market account to ensure that you can afford it; check in with various retailers and compare prices. When you set out to make a purchase, only buy what's on your list.

WARNING

The internet can be a time-efficient tool for performing research and price comparisons, but be careful of common online problems. The first is advertising that masquerades as informative articles. The second problem is small online retailers who may be here today and gone tomorrow or who may be unresponsive after the purchase. Finally, internet retailers are adept at pushing additional items that they have good reason to believe will appeal to you, given your other purchases.

>> **Always look for the best values for products purchased.** Value means the level of quality given the price paid for the

item. Don't assume that a more expensive or brand-name product is better, because you often don't get what you pay for. Overpaying for products isn't how you build wealth.

>> **Reduce time spent on earning and spending money.** The saddest part about being on the work and consumption treadmill is how much of your time and life you may occupy earning and then spending money. Consider how many hours you spend working and shopping in a typical week. In addition to the time actually spent at work, consider commute time and time spent getting dressed and prepared for work. Now add in all the time you spend shopping and buying things. Compare the grand total of time spent on work- and shopping-related activities to time spent on the things you really enjoy in life. Think of building wealth in terms of increasing your freedom and the time you're able to spend on the things you enjoy.

>> **Make saving money a habit.** Just as with changing what you eat or your exercise routine (or lack thereof), modifying your spending and savings habits is easier said than done. The information that follows can help motivate you and get you on the path to consistently saving and then investing your money wisely to achieve your desired goals.

TIP

Try brainstorming a list of five luxuries that you currently spend some money on that you may consider doing without. Your list might include things like morning Starbucks lattes, salon hair products, or Friday night at the movies. Pick one or two items from the list that you would be most comfortable going without and then see how you feel about that change before possibly considering eliminating other spending.

Living within your means

Spending too much is a *relative* problem. Two people can each spend $50,000 per year (including their taxes) yet still have drastically different financial circumstances. How? Suppose that one of them earns $60,000 annually, while the other makes $45,000. The $60,000 income earner saves $10,000 each year. The $45,000 wage earner, on the other hand, accumulates $5,000 of new debt (or spends that amount from prior savings). So, spend within your means. If you do nothing else from this chapter, please be sure to do this!

Don't let the spending habits of others dictate yours. Certain people — and you know who they are — bring out the big spender in you. Do something else with them besides shopping and spending. If you can't find any other activity to share with them, try shopping with limited cash and no credit cards. That way, you can't overspend on impulse.

How much you can safely spend while working toward your financial goals depends on what your goals are and where you are financially. Save first for your goals and then live on what's left over.

Turning your back on consumer credit

Buying items that depreciate — such as cars, clothing, and vacations — on credit is hazardous to your long-term financial health. Buy only what you can afford today. If you'll be forced to carry a debt for months or years on end, you can't really afford what you're buying on credit today.

WARNING

Without a doubt, *renting-to-own* is the most expensive way to buy. Here's how it works: You see a huge ad blaring "$19.99 for a 65-inch Smart TV!" Well, the ad has a big hitch: That's $19.99 per week, for many weeks. When all is said and done (and paid), buying a $489 65-inch Smart TV through a rent-to-own store costs a typical buyer more than $1,800! Welcome to the world of rent-to-own stores, which offer cash-poor consumers the ability to lease consumer items and, at the end of the lease, an option to buy.

If you think that paying an 18 percent interest rate on a credit card is expensive, consider this: The effective interest rate charged on many rent-to-own purchases exceeds 100 percent; in some cases, it may be 200 percent or more! Renting-to-own makes buying on a credit card look like a deal. I'm not sharing this information to encourage you to buy using credit over time on credit cards but to point out what a rip-off renting-to-own is. Such stores prey on cashless consumers who either can't get credit cards or don't understand how expensive renting-to-own really is. Forget the instant gratification and save a set amount each week until you can afford what you want.

Consumer credit is expensive, and it reinforces a bad financial habit: spending more than you can afford.

REMEMBER

Repaying your debt

The *best* way to reduce the costs of consumer debt is to avoid it in the first place when you're making consumption purchases. You can avoid consumer debt by eliminating your access to credit or by limiting your purchase of consumer items to what you can pay off each month. Borrow only for long-term investments, like a home, real estate, and education.

Don't keep a credit card that charges you an annual fee, especially if you pay your balance in full each month. Many no-fee credit cards exist — and some even offer you a reward/benefit for using them:

>> **Discover Card** (phone 800-347-2683; website www.discover.com) offers rebates of 1 percent of purchases (higher percentage offered for some particular retailers) in cash. At the end of your first year, Discover automatically matches an unlimited amount of the cash back you've earned that year.

>> **Fidelity Rewards Visa** (phone 888-325-6196; www.fidelity.com/cash-management/visa-signature-card) pays unlimited 2 percent cash back on all purchases, and that cash is deposited monthly into an eligible Fidelity account such as a cash management account, IRA, and so forth.

>> **USAA Preferred Cash Rewards** (phone 800-922-9092; website www.usaa.com) offers 1.5 percent cash back on purchases for members of the military and their immediate relatives.

Consider the cards in the preceding list only if you pay your balance in full each month, because no-fee cards typically don't offer the lowest interest rates for balances carried from month to month. The small rewards that you earn really won't do you much good if they're negated by high interest charges.

TIP

If you have a credit card that charges an annual fee, try calling the company and saying that you want to cancel the card because you can get a competitor's card without an annual fee. Many banks will agree to waive the fee on the spot. Some require you to call back yearly to cancel the fee — a hassle that can be avoided by getting a true no-fee card.

Some cards that charge an annual fee and offer credits toward the purchase of a specific item, such as a car, airline ticket, or hotel stay, may be worth your while if you pay your bill in full each month and charge $10,000 or more annually. *Note:* Be careful — you may be tempted to charge more on a card that rewards you for more purchases. Spending more in order to rack up bonuses defeats the purpose of the credits.

Avoiding the "More Money, More Stuff" Trap

What you spend your money on is sometimes a matter of habit rather than a matter of what you really want or value. For example, some people shop at whatever stores are close to them. These days, some people order many things online, which can lead to overspending as well.

It's one thing to want to reduce your spending and quite another to actually do it. Sloppiness in our spending more typically happens when times are good and money is more plentiful. But to build wealth, you need to reduce spending to increase savings even when times are good, and this requires working on your habits.

TIP

Small changes to your habits can go a long way toward eliminating fat from your spending diet. For example, you can save money by buying in bulk. Some stores specialize in selling larger packages or quantities of a product at a lower price because they save money on the packaging and handling. If you're single, shop with a friend and split the bulk purchases. You can also do some comparison shopping online, but be sure you're surveying reputable websites that stand behind what they sell and that provide high-quality customer service.

The following sections highlight proven ways to trim spending and boost your savings as you pursue your wealth-building goals. You can cherry-pick those that you are more interested in trying. Consider not just where you spend your money, but where you spend your time — and the changes you want to make.

Housing expenses

For most people, the money that they spend on shelter is their single largest expenditure (or second biggest behind taxes). In addition to your monthly mortgage payment, property taxes, and homeowner's insurance, other home-related expenses include maintenance of the home, commuting costs, and educational and other expenses for your children, given the amenities and services of the community.

There are various strategies to reduce your homeownership expenses:

>> **Spend less on a home.** What do you do if you already own a home that is stretching your finances thin? Many people think of their housing expenses as fixed. It's not true in the vast majority of cases. After weighing the costs of selling and buying, you may want to consider a move to a less-expensive area or residence.

>> **Keep an eye on interest rates.** If they fall at least 1 percent from the level at which you bought, consider the costs and benefits of refinancing.

>> **Check on property value.** If property prices in your area have been falling, you may be able to appeal to lower your property's assessed value and reduce your property taxes.

>> **Consider a renter.** In the spirit of brainstorming ideas, perhaps you could stay in your current home but find ways to bring in some rental income to help offset some of your costs. You could take in a longer-term renter, for example. This may be more palatable if your home can have a self-contained area/unit for the renter.

REMEMBER

If you are currently a renter, you may consider moving to a less-expensive rental or into a shared rental. Living alone certainly has its advantages, but it is expensive. Also, consider eventually buying a property. It may seem counterintuitive but being a renter can be quite expensive. Think long-term: As a property owner, someday your mortgage will eventually be paid off. In the meantime, a fixed-rate mortgage payment doesn't increase over the years. Your rent, on the other hand, does generally increase with the cost of living or inflation.

Lowering your energy costs

Escalating energy prices remind all of us how much we depend upon and use oil, electricity, and natural gas in our daily lives. A number of terrific websites are packed with suggestions and tips for how to lower your energy costs. Before I present those to you, however, here are the basics:

>> **Drive fuel-efficient cars and drive efficiently.** If you're safety minded, you know how dangerous driving can be and aren't willing to risk your life driving a pint-size vehicle just to get 50 miles per gallon. That said, you can drive safe cars that are fuel-efficient. Also, take it easy on the gas pedal and brakes; accelerate and brake gradually, and don't speed on the highway because doing so gobbles more fuel. Although it varies based on the type of car you drive and your driving habits, each 5 mph you drive over 60 mph can reduce your fuel economy by about 7 percent.

>> **Be thrifty at home.** Get all family members on the same page, without driving them crazy, to turn off lights they don't need. Turn down the heat at night, which saves money and helps you sleep better, and turn it down when no one is home. *Hint:* If people are walking around your home during the winter with shorts on (as happens in too many college dormitories) instead of wearing sweatpants, turn the heat down!

>> **Service and maintain what you have.** Anything that uses energy — from your cars to your furnace — should be regularly serviced. For instance, make sure you clean your filters.

>> **Investigate energy efficiency before you buy.** This advice applies not only to appliances but also to an entire home. Some builders are building energy efficiency into their new homes.

TIP

My favorite energy information and tip websites are the Database of State Incentives for Renewables & Efficiency (www.dsireusa.org) and the U.S. Department of Energy's energy-saving tips (www.energy.gov/energysaver/energy-saver).

Trimming your taxes

Taxes are probably one of your largest — if not *the* largest — expenditures. For most people, taxes are typically their second largest expense category after housing. Reducing your taxes generally requires some advance planning. Making sound financial decisions involves considering tax and other financial ramifications. Don't wait until you're ready to file your tax return to find out how to reduce your tax burden. Please see Chapter 7 for strategies to lower your taxes.

Retirement savings plans are one of the best and simplest ways to reduce your tax burden. (I explain more about retirement savings plans in Chapter 8.) Unfortunately, most people can't take full advantage of these plans because they spend everything they make. So not only do they have less savings, but they also pay higher income taxes — a double whammy.

I've attended many presentations where a fast-talking investment guy in an expensive suit lectures about the importance of saving for retirement and explains how to invest your savings. Yet details and tips about finding the money to save (the hard part for most people) are left to the imagination.

REMEMBER

In order to take advantage of the tax savings that come through retirement savings plans, you must first spend less than you earn. Only then can you afford to contribute to these plans. That's why the majority of this chapter is about strategies to reduce your spending.

Reduced sales tax is another benefit of spending less and saving more. When you buy most consumer products and services, you pay sales tax. Therefore, when you spend less money and save more in retirement accounts, you reduce your income and sales taxes. (See Chapter 7 for detailed tax-reduction strategies.)

Keeping an eye on insurance premiums

Insurance fills a vital and useful role. You don't want to be in the position of absorbing a financial catastrophe. That's why, for example, you want adequate homeowner's and health insurance.

Beyond essential coverage, there's no need to waste money on insurance. Many people overspend on insurance by purchasing coverage that's unnecessary or that covers small potential losses (such as when shipping a $100 or $200 item).

The following list explains the most common ways people waste money on insurance:

TIP

» **Keeping low deductibles.** The *deductible* is the amount of a loss that must come out of your pocket. For example, if you have an auto insurance policy with a $100 collision deductible and you get into an accident, you pay for the first $100 of damage, and your insurance company picks up the rest. Low deductibles, however, translate into much higher premiums for you. In the long run, you save money with a higher deductible, even when factoring in the potential for greater out-of-pocket costs to you when you do have a claim. Insurance should protect you from economic disaster. Don't get carried away with a really high deductible, which can cause financial hardship if you have a claim and lack savings.

If you have a lot of claims, you won't come out ahead with lower deductibles, because your insurance premiums will escalate. Plus, low deductibles mean more claim forms to file for small losses (creating more hassle). Filing an insurance claim usually isn't an enjoyable or quick experience.

» **Covering small potential losses.** You shouldn't buy insurance for anything that won't be a financial catastrophe if you have to pay for it out of your own pocket. Although the postal service isn't perfect, insuring inexpensive gifts sent in the mail isn't worth the price. Buying dental or home warranty plans, which also cover relatively small potential expenditures, doesn't make financial sense for the same reason.

» **Failing to shop around.** Rates vary *tremendously* from insurer to insurer.

Managing medical expenses

Examine your employer's benefit plans. Take advantage of being able to put away a portion of your income before taxes to pay for out-of-pocket healthcare expenses. Make sure that you pay close attention to the "use it or lose it" provisions of some plans.

Shop around when seeking health insurance. Don't take any one physician's advice as gospel. Always get a second opinion for any major surgery. Have a frank talk with your therapist about how much total time and money you can expect to spend and what kind of results you can expect to receive. And investigate alternative treatment for some forms of chronic pain or disease — alternative medicine may lead to better *and* lower-cost healthcare.

If you have to take certain drugs on an ongoing basis and pay for them out of pocket, ordering through a mail-order company can bring down your costs and help make refilling your prescriptions more convenient. Ask your health plan provider for more information about this option. Also inquire about generic versions of drugs. Websites and apps like GoodRx can help you save money on prescriptions, though it can mean going to different drugstores for the best price on different prescriptions.

Spending less on cars and transportation

When you buy a car, research what the car is worth. The dealer markup, especially on new cars, can be substantial. Numerous publications and services such as Consumer Reports (www.consumer reports.org), Kelley Blue Book (www.kbb.com), and Edmunds (www.edmunds.com) provide this information. Before you purchase, also consider insurance costs of the different makes and models you're considering. Before committing to buy a particular make and model, call auto insurers to shop for insurance quotes, as rates vary greatly and should factor into your purchase decision.

Avoid taking an auto loan or lease. The seemingly reasonable monthly payment amount of loans and leases deludes people into spending more on a car than they can really afford. In the long term, paying with cash is less costly.

If you owe on an auto loan, consider selling that car if you can manage without it. Getting out of an auto lease before its official end is more challenging. Two websites — www.swapalease.com and www.leasetrader.com — help match folks looking to exit a lease early with people interested in taking over a lease. You can also contact local dealers to see if they'd be interested in buying the car from you.

TIP

Also take a hard look at whether you need a car. Although living in a particular community may appear to save you money, it may not if it requires you to have a car because of the lack of other transportation options such as public transit or the distance from work.

Considering kid-related expenses

Childcare is often a major expense for parents of young kids. For some people, this is a necessity; for others, this is a choice. Check that your analysis of what you earn from your work and what you spend on childcare makes sense.

TIP

Help your children develop good habits from a young age. Share with them the realities of your family's finances and involve them when setting limits on purchases and activities — this will help them to find out about financial responsibility and obligations and why you shouldn't purchase every item advertised on TV.

Saving on food and dining

Eating in restaurants is costly, particularly if you're not careful about where and what you eat. When you do eat out, to keep costs down, minimize the alcohol and desserts, which can greatly increase the cost of a meal and undermine its nutritional value. Also try going out more for lunch rather than dinner, which is usually more expensive. Or even better, learn to cook at home.

Regarding groceries, try to keep a decent inventory of things at home (but don't go overboard with perishables, which you may end up tossing out if you don't use them in time). This will minimize trips to the store and the need to dine out for lack of options at home. Try to do most of your shopping through discount warehouse-type stores, which offer low prices for buying in bulk, or grocery stores that offer bulk purchases or discount prices. If you live alone, don't be deterred — find a friend to share the large purchases with you.

Reducing phone bills

Thanks to increased competition and technology, telephoning costs continue to fall. If you haven't looked for lower rates in recent years, you're probably paying more than you need to for quality phone service. Unfortunately, shopping among the many service providers is difficult. Plans come with different restrictions, minimums, and bells and whistles.

TIP

You may have to switch companies to reduce your bill, but some people can save with their current phone company simply by getting onto a better calling plan. Contact your current provider(s) and ask them which of their calling plans offers the lowest cost for you based on the patterns of your calls.

Shopping for technology

We have email, smartphones, voice mail, tablets, satellite TV, the internet, streaming services, virtual reality devices, and too many other ways to stay in touch and entertained 24/7. Visit a store that sells electronics, and you'll find no end to new gadgets.

REMEMBER

If you're prone to compulsive shopping and decisions, the worst way to shop for electronics and technology-based products is to wander around stores selling lots of these goods while a salesperson pitches you things. You may be prone to quick buying decisions online as well if you're comfortable clicking and buying on websites. Educate yourself (check out Consumer Reports and CNET's website at www.cnet.com) to determine what you really need and what provides the best value.

Finding affordable recreation and entertainment

Think of ways to substitute activities to reduce spending without reducing your enjoyment. Exchange invitations with friends to cook dinner at home rather than going out to restaurants. Don't be shy about using coupons or special offers at restaurants you normally frequent. Find friends to visit when you travel. Attend a matinee movie instead of one during the high-priced evening hours. Many of the most enjoyable things in life — time spent with family and friends, outdoor activities, and so on — don't have to cost much or even any money at all.

Reducing clothing expenses

Avoid the temptation to buy new clothes for a new season or to use shopping as a hobby. If you enjoy the visual stimulation, go window shopping and leave all forms of payment at home. (Carrying a small amount of cash is fine!) Avoid fashions that are trendy and that you won't wear after the trend moves on. Minimize clothing that requires dry cleaning, which is costly and exposes your body to unnecessary and unhealthy chemicals.

TIP

Go to your closet or jewelry box and tally up the loot. What else could you have done with all that spent cash? Do you see things you regret buying or forgot you even had? Don't make the same mistake again. If you have a lot of stuff that you don't want, try selling items through local consignment stores or online through Poshmark, RealReal, Kidizen, and eBay. Return recent unused purchases to stores. For older items you have no intention of using anymore, try a consignment store to realize some cash back or try donating to a charity if you are able to itemize your deductions by filing Schedule A with your IRS Form 1040.

Paying for hair care and other personal-care services

At the prices charged by some of the trendy hair places, you have to really adore what they do to justify the price. Consider going periodically to a no-frills stylist for maintenance after getting a fabulous cut at a more expensive place. If you're daring, you can try getting your hair cut at a local training school.

TIP

For parents of young children, buying simple-to-use home hair-cutting electric clippers (such as Wahl's) can be a great time- and money-saver — no more agonizing trips with little ones to have their hair cut by a "stranger." The kit pays for itself after just two haircuts!

Having regular facials, pedicures, and manicures can add up quickly. In fact, the difference in high prices for cosmetics in department stores and cosmetic stores like Ulta and Sephora over dramatically lower prices in discount stores like Walmart and drugstores like Walgreens and CVS can add up quickly in savings.

Reducing health club expenses

You don't have to belong to a trendy club to receive the benefits of exercise. Local schools, colleges, and universities often have tennis courts, running tracks, swimming pools, basketball courts, and exercise rooms, and they may provide instruction as well. Community centers offer fitness programs and classes, too. Metropolitan areas that have lots of health clubs undoubtedly have the widest range of options and prices. *Note:* When figuring the cost of membership, be sure to factor in the cost of travel to and from the club, as well as any parking costs (and the realistic likelihood of going there regularly to work out).

Don't forget that healthy exercise can be done indoors or out, free of charge. Isn't hiking in the park or playing tennis or pickleball outside on a warm day more fun than pedaling away on a stationary bike, anyway? You may want to buy some basic gym equipment for use at home. Be careful, though: Lots of exercise equipment gathers dust at home.

Buying gifts

Think about how you approach buying gifts throughout the year — especially during the holidays. As with other purchases you make, paying careful attention to where and what you buy can save you significant dollars. Don't make the mistake of equating the value of a gift with its dollar cost.

TIP

And here's a good suggestion for getting rid of those old, unwanted gifts: a *white elephant* gift exchange. Everyone brings a wrapped, unwanted gift from the past and exchanges it with someone else. After the gifts are opened, trading is allowed. (Just be sure not to bring a gift that was given to you by any of the exchange participants!) Can't be bothered with this? Consider donating unwanted items for a tax write-off if you itemize on Schedule A.

Charitable contributions

Did you know that Americans are among the most giving people on Earth? That said, your charitable contributions are part of your budget, and as such, should be reviewed. To take into account how charitable contributions can affect your taxes, see Chapter 7.

Vacations

Try taking short vacations that are close to home. Have you been to a state or national park recently? Great places that you've always wanted to see but haven't visited for one reason or another are probably located within 200 miles of you. Or you may want to just block out some time and do what family pets do: Relax around your home and enjoy some naps.

If you do travel a long way to a popular destination, travel during the off-season for the best deals on airfares and hotels. Keep an eye out for discounts. The *Consumer Reports Travel* newsletter and numerous websites, such as www.priceline.com, www.expedia.com, and www.travelocity.com can help you find low-cost travel options as well. Seniors generally qualify for special fares at most airlines — ask the airline what programs it offers.

Also, be sure to shop around, even when working with travel agents/advisors. Travel agents work on commission, so they may not work hard to find you the best deals. Tour packages, when they meet your interests and needs, may save you money.

Paring down professional expenses

Accountants, lawyers, and financial advisors can be worth their expense if they're good. But be wary of professionals who create or perpetuate work and have conflicts of interest with their recommendations.

Make sure that you get organized before meeting with professionals for tax, legal, or financial advice. Do some background research to evaluate their strengths and biases. Set goals and estimate fees in advance so you know what you're getting yourself into.

Computer-based and other resources can be useful, low-cost alternatives and supplements to hiring professionals.

Costly addictions

Human beings are creatures of habit. Everybody has habits they wish they didn't have, and breaking those habits can be very difficult. Costly habits are the worst. Kick the smoking habit, and find help to stop abusing alcohol and other drugs.

TIP

The Substance Abuse and Mental Health Services Administration (phone 800-662-4357 or 800-662-HELP; www.samhsa.gov/) can refer you to local drug treatment programs and programs such as Alcoholics Anonymous. It also provides information and literature about the various types of substance abuse. Access their online treatment locator at findtreatment.gov.

Gambling

The house *always* comes out ahead in the long run. Why do you think so many governments run lotteries? Because governments make big money on people who gamble, that's why. Casinos, horse and dog racetracks, and other gambling establishments are sure long-term losers for you. So, too, is the short-term trading of stocks, which isn't investing but gambling. Getting hooked on the dream of winning is easy. And sure, occasionally you win a little bit (just enough to keep you coming back). Every now and then, a few folks win a lot. But your hard-earned capital mostly winds up in the pockets of the casino owners.

If you gamble just for entertainment, take only what you can afford to lose. Gamblers Anonymous (phone 909-931-9056; website www.gamblersanonymous.org) helps those for whom gambling has become an addiction.

Budgeting: Yes, You Need a Financial Plan

When most people hear the word *budgeting*, they think unpleasant thoughts — like those associated with *dieting* — and rightfully so. But budgeting can help you move from knowing how much you spend on various things to successfully reducing your spending. Over time, budgeting can also help you improve your habits and build wealth.

The first step in the process of *budgeting*, or planning your future spending, is to analyze where your current spending is going. After you do that, calculate how much more you'd like to save each month. Then comes the hard part: deciding where to make cuts in your spending. The earlier section "Avoiding the 'More Money, More Stuff' Trap" offers some ideas to get you started.

Suppose that you're currently not saving any of your monthly income and you want to save 10 percent for retirement. If you can save and invest through a tax-sheltered retirement account — for example, a 401(k), 403(b), or a SEP-IRA — you don't actually need to cut your spending by 10 percent to reach a savings goal of 10 percent (of your gross income). When you contribute money to a tax-deductible retirement account, you reduce your federal and state taxes. If you're a moderate-income-earner paying, say, 30 percent in federal and state taxes on your marginal income, you actually need to reduce your spending by only 7 percent to save 10 percent. The other 3 percent of the savings comes from the lowering of your taxes. (The higher your tax bracket, the less you need to cut your spending to reach a particular savings goal.)

So, to boost your savings rate to 10 percent, go through your current spending category by category until you come up with enough proposed cuts to reduce your spending by 7 percent. Make your cuts in the areas that will be the least painful and where you're getting the least value from your current level of spending. (If you don't have access to a tax-deductible retirement account, budgeting still involves the same process of assessment and making cuts in various spending categories, but your cuts need to add up to the entire amount you want to save, in this example, 10 percent rather than 7 percent.)

Another method of budgeting involves starting completely from scratch rather than examining your current expenses and making cuts from that starting point. Ask yourself how much you'd like to spend on different categories. The advantage of this approach is that it doesn't allow your current spending levels to constrain your thinking. You'll likely be amazed at the discrepancies between what you think you should be spending and what you actually are spending in certain categories.

Chapter 3

Exploring Winning Investment Strategies

Making wise investments need not be complicated. However, many investors get bogged down in the morass of the thousands of investment choices out there and the often-conflicting perspectives on how to invest. This chapter helps you grasp the important "bigger picture" issues that can help you ensure that your investment plan meshes with your needs and the realities of the investment marketplace.

Compound Interest: The Eighth Wonder of the World

Before you select a specific investment, first determine your investment needs and goals. Why are you saving money — what are you going to use it for? You don't need to earmark every dollar, but you should set some major objectives or goals. Establishing goals is important because the expected use of the money helps you determine how long to invest it. And that, in turn, helps you determine which investments to choose.

The risk level of your investments should factor in your time frame and your comfort level. Investing in high-risk vehicles doesn't make sense if you'll need to spend the funds within the next few years or if you'll have to spend all your profits on stress-induced medical bills! For example, suppose you've been accumulating money for a down payment on a home you want to buy in a few years. You can't afford much risk with that money because you're going to need it sooner rather than later. Putting that money in the stock market, then, is foolish. The stock market can drop a lot in a year or over several years. So, stocks are probably too risky a place to invest money you plan to use soon.

Perhaps you're saving toward a longer-term goal, such as retirement, that's 20 or 30 years away. In this case, you're in a position to make riskier investments, because your holdings have more time to bounce back from temporary losses or setbacks. You may want to consider investing in growth investments, such as stocks, within a retirement account that you leave alone for 20 years or longer. You can tolerate year-to-year volatility in the market — you have time on your side.

Understanding the primary investments

For a moment, forget all the buzzwords, jargon, and product names you've heard tossed around in the investment world — in many cases, they obscure, sometimes intentionally, what an investment really is and hide the hefty fees and commissions.

Imagine a world with only two investment flavors — think of chocolate and vanilla ice cream (or low-fat frozen yogurt for you health-minded folks). The investment world is really just as simple. You have only two major investment choices: You can be a lender or an owner.

Looking at lending investments

You're a lender when you invest your money in a bank certificate of deposit (CD), a Treasury bill, or a bond issued by a company like Home Depot, for example. In each case, you lend your money to an organization — a bank, the federal government, or Home Depot. You're paid an agreed-upon rate of interest for lending your money. The organization also promises to have your original investment (the *principal*) returned to you on a specific date.

Getting paid all the interest in addition to your original investment (as promised) is the best that can happen with a lending investment. Given that the investment landscape is littered with carcasses of failed investments, this is not a result to take for granted!

Here are the drawbacks of lending investments:

>> **Broken promises:** You don't get everything you were promised. Promises can be broken under extenuating circumstances. When a company goes bankrupt, for example, you can lose all or part of your original investment.

>> **Inflation:** Even if you get what you were promised, inflation may reduce the purchasing power of your money. Higher inflation returned for the first time in a long time in the aftermath of the COVID-19 pandemic and associated spending and shutdowns. Also, the value of a bond may drop below what you paid for it if interest rates rise or the quality/risk of the issuing company declines.

>> **Low fixed rate of return:** Some investors make the common mistake of thinking that they're diversifying their long-term investment money by buying several bonds, some CDs, and an annuity. The problem, however, is that all these investments pay a relatively low fixed rate of return that's exposed to the vagaries of inflation.

>> **Limited principal and interest:** You don't share in the success of the organization to which you lend your money. If the company doubles or triples in size and profits, your principal and interest rate don't double or triple in size along with it; they stay the same. Of course, such success does ensure that you'll get your promised interest and principal.

Exploring ownership investments

You're an *owner* when you invest your money in an asset, such as a company or real estate, that can generate earnings or profits. Here are some examples of ownership investments:

>> **Stock ownership:** As a stockholder, you do share in the profits of a company in the form of annual dividends and an increase (you hope) in the stock price if the company grows and becomes more profitable.

>> **Real estate:** Real estate can produce profits when it's rented out for more than the expense of owning the property or sold at a price higher than what you paid for it. In Chapter 6, I cover building wealth through real estate investing.

>> **Small business:** To invest in small business, you can start your own business, buy and operate an existing business, or simply invest in promising small businesses. In Chapter 5, I describe how to build wealth by investing in small business.

Shunning gambling and "get rich quick" vehicles

Although investing is often risky, it's not gambling. *Gambling* is putting your money into schemes that are sure to lose you money over time. That's not to say that everyone loses or that you lose every time you gamble. However, the deck is stacked against you. The house wins most of the time.

WARNING

Casinos and lotteries are set up to pay out 50 to 60 cents on the dollar. The rest goes to profits and covering those businesses' operating costs. Sure, you may win a bet or two, but in the long run, you're almost guaranteed to lose about 40 to 50 percent of what you bet. Would you put your money in an "investment" where your expected return over the long term was negative 40 percent?

Historically, the best wealth-building investments have returned an average of about 8 to 9 percent per year. You should keep that number in mind as you evaluate seemingly attractive alternatives with the belief that you will double or triple your investment in a year or less.

Here are gambling and "get rich quick" vehicles to avoid:

>> **Futures, options, and other derivatives:** Futures, options, and commodity futures are *derivatives* or financial investments whose value is derived from the performance of another security, such as a stock or bond. These risky investments rely on short-term market movements; as with gambling, you might occasionally win, but you can also lose it all.

>> **Day trading:** *Day trading* — which is the rapid buying and selling of securities online — is an equally foolish vehicle for individual investors. This is speculation and gambling, not investing. And even if you're using a broker who offers "free" trading, every time you buy and sell, you're effectively paying a fee given the inevitable spread between the buy and sell price for a given security.

Frequent trading also increases your tax bill as profits realized over short time periods are taxed at your highest possible tax rate. You can certainly make some profits when day trading. However, over an extended period of time, you'll inevitably underperform the broad market averages. In those rare instances where you may do a little better than the market averages, the profits are rarely worth the time and personal sacrifices that you, your family, and your friendships endure.

>> **Get rich quick schemes:** If it sounds too good to be true, it probably is. In today's high-tech world, people are bombarded from all directions — mailers, social media ads, radio and podcast commercials, and on and on — on ways to make money, fast. I'm here to tell you that getting rich quick is more of a pipe dream than an investment strategy. Investing for the long term is the way to grow your money.

>> **Cryptocurrencies:** Cryptocurrencies represent another "get rich quick" scheme. Websites and social media have recounted tales of folks becoming rich over short time periods after buying into a particular cryptocurrency like Bitcoin and Ethereum that zoomed skyward. As many inexperienced and naïve investors who were lured into cryptocurrencies discovered, many of these cryptocurrencies have ended up being poor investments.

Understanding investment returns

During this past century, ownership investments such as stocks and investment real estate returned around 9 percent per year, handily beating lending investments such as bonds (around 5 percent) and savings accounts (roughly 4 percent) in the investment performance race. Inflation has averaged 3 percent per year.

If you already know that the stock market can be risky, you may be wondering why investing in stocks is worth the anxiety and potential losses. Why bother for a few extra percent per year? Well, over many years, a few extra percent per year can really magnify the growth of your money (see Table 3-1). The more years you have to invest, the greater the difference a few percent makes in your returns.

TABLE 3-1 **The Difference a Few Percent Makes**

At This Rate of Return on $10,000 Invested	You'll Have This Much in 25 Years	You'll Have This Much in 40 Years
4% (savings account)	$26,658	$48,010
5% (bond)	$33,863	$70,400
9% (stocks and investment real estate)	$86,231	$314,094

REMEMBER

Investing is not a spectator sport. You can't earn good returns on stocks and real estate if you keep your money in cash on the sidelines. If you invest in growth investments such as stocks and real estate, don't chase one new investment after another trying to beat the market average returns. *The biggest value comes from being in the market, not from beating it.*

Leaving you with some final advice

Here are several other issues to keep in mind as you make important investing choices:

>> **Don't invest based on sales solicitations.** Companies that advertise and solicit prospective customers aggressively offer some of the worst financial products with the highest fees. The companies with the best investment offerings get plenty of new business through the word-of-mouth recommendations of satisfied customers.

>> **Don't invest in what you don't understand.** When you don't understand an investment, odds are good that it won't be right for you. Before you invest in anything, you need to know its track record, its true costs, and how liquid (easily convertible to cash) it is.

>> **Minimize fees.** Avoid investments that carry high sales commissions and management expenses (usually disclosed in a prospectus). Higher-fee investments, on average, perform worse than alternatives with lower fees. High ongoing management fees often go toward lavish offices, glossy brochures, and skyscraper salaries, or toward propping up small, inefficient operations.

>> **Pay attention to tax consequences.** Even if you never become an investment expert, you're smart enough to know that the more money you pay in taxes, the less you have for investing and playing with. See Chapter 8 for info on how retirement accounts can help boost your investment returns. For investments outside retirement accounts, you need to match the types of investments to your tax situation.

Exploring Bonds and Other Lending Investments

You can invest in bonds in one of two major ways: You can purchase individual bonds, or you can invest in a professionally selected and managed portfolio of bonds via a bond mutual fund or exchange-traded fund.

Deciding between individual bonds and bond funds

Unless the bonds you're considering purchasing are easy to analyze and homogeneous (such as Treasury bonds), you're generally better off investing in bonds through a mutual fund or exchange-traded fund. Here's why:

>> **Diversification is more difficult with individual bonds.** You shouldn't put your money into a small number of bonds of companies in the same industry or that mature at the same time. It's difficult to cost-effectively build a diversified bond portfolio with individual issues unless you have a substantial amount of money ($1 million) that you want to invest in bonds.

>> **Individual bonds cost you more money.** If you purchase individual bonds through a broker, you're going to pay a commission. Investing in bonds through a fund is more cost-effective. Great bond funds are yours for less than 0.5 percent per year in operating expenses. Selecting good bond funds isn't hard, as I explain later in this chapter.

>> **You've got better things to do with your time.** Do you really want to research bonds and go bond shopping? Bonds and the companies that stand behind them aren't that simple to understand. After you purchase a bond, you need to do the same things that a good bond mutual fund portfolio manager needs to do, such as track the issuer's creditworthiness and monitor other important financial developments.

Obtaining bond prices

Business-focused publications and websites provide daily bond pricing. You may also call a broker or browse websites to obtain bond prices. In addition to the direction of overall interest rates, changes in the financial health of the issuing entity that stands behind the bond strongly affect the price of an individual bond.

Purchasing Treasuries

If you want to purchase Treasury bonds, buying them through the Treasury Direct program is the lowest-cost option. Call 800-722-2678 or visit the U.S. Department of Treasury's website (www.treasurydirect.gov).

You may also purchase and hold Treasury bonds through brokerage firms and mutual funds. Brokers typically charge a flat fee for buying a Treasury bond. Buying Treasuries through a brokerage account makes sense if you hold other securities through the brokerage account and you like the ability to quickly sell a Treasury bond that you hold. Selling Treasury bonds held through Treasury Direct requires you to transfer the bonds to a broker.

REMEMBER

The advantage of a fund that invests in Treasuries is that it typically holds Treasuries of differing maturities, thus offering diversification. You can generally buy and sell *no-load* (commission-free) Treasury bond mutual funds easily and without fees. Funds, however, do charge an ongoing management fee.

Shopping for other individual bonds

Purchasing other types of individual bonds, such as corporate and mortgage bonds, is a much more treacherous and time-consuming undertaking than buying Treasuries. Here's my advice for doing it right and minimizing the chance of mistakes:

>> **Don't buy through salespeople.** Brokerage firms that employ representatives on commission are in the sales business. Many of the worst bond-investing disasters have befallen customers of such brokerage firms. Your best bet is to purchase individual bonds through discount brokers.

>> **Don't be suckered into high yields — buy quality.** Yes, junk bonds pay higher yields, but they also have a much higher chance of default. Nothing personal, but you're not going to do as good a job as a professional money manager at spotting problems and red flags. Stick with highly rated bonds so you don't have to worry about and suffer through these consequences. Lower-rated bonds got clobbered during the 2007–08 financial crisis and again during the 2020 COVID-19 pandemic.

>> **Understand that bonds may be called early.** Many bonds, especially corporate bonds, can legally be called before maturity. In this case, the bond issuer pays you back early because it doesn't need to borrow as much money or because interest rates have fallen, and the borrower wants to reissue new bonds at a lower interest rate. Be especially careful about purchasing bonds that were issued at higher interest rates than those that currently prevail. Borrowers pay off such bonds first.

>> **Diversify.** To buffer changes in the economy that adversely affect one industry or a few industries more than others, invest in and hold bonds from a variety of companies in different industries.

TIP

Of the money that you want to invest in bonds, don't put more than 5 percent into any one bond; that means you need to hold at least 20 bonds. Diversification requires a good amount to invest, given the size of most bonds, and because trading fees erode your investment balance if you invest too little. If you can't achieve this level of diversification, use a bond mutual fund or exchange-traded fund.

>> **Shop around.** Just like when you buy a car, shop around for good prices on the bonds that you have in mind. The hard part is doing an apples-to-apples comparison because different brokers may not offer the same exact bonds. Remember that the two biggest determinants of what a bond should yield are its maturity date and its credit rating.

TIP

Unless you invest in boring, simple-to-understand bonds such as Treasuries, you're better off investing in bonds via the best bond mutual funds. One exception is if you absolutely, positively must receive your principal back on a certain date. Because bond funds don't mature, individual bonds with the correct maturity for you may best suit your needs. Consider Treasuries because they carry such a low default risk. Otherwise, you need a lot of time, money, and patience to invest well in individual bonds.

If you already own individual bonds and they fit your financial objectives and tax situation, you can hold them until maturity because you already incurred a commission when they were purchased; selling them now would just create an additional fee. When the bonds mature, the broker who sold them to you will probably be more than happy to sell you some more. That's the time to check out good bond mutual funds.

Don't mistakenly think that individual bonds you already own pay the yield that they had when they were originally issued. (That yield is the number listed in the name of the bond on your brokerage account statement.) As the market level of interest rates changes, the effective *yield* (the interest payment divided by the bond's price) on your bonds fluctuates to rise and fall with the market level of rates for similar bonds. So, if rates have fallen since you bought your bonds, the value of those bonds has increased — which, in turn, reduces the effective yield that you're earning on your invested dollars.

Considering other lending investments

Bonds, money market funds, and bank savings vehicles are hardly the only lending investments. A variety of companies are more than willing to have you lend them your money and pay you a relatively fixed rate of interest. In many cases, though, you're better off staying away from these investments, especially *guaranteed-investment contracts* (GICs) and *private mortgages*, sometimes called *second mortgages*, which resemble the ones you take out to purchase a home.

WARNING

Too many investors get sucked into lending investments that offer higher yields. Always remember: A low-risk, high-yield investment doesn't exist. Earning a relatively high interest rate goes hand in hand with accepting relatively high risk.

If you're willing to lend your money to borrowers who carry a relatively high risk of defaulting, consider investing in high-yield (junk) bond mutual funds instead. With these funds, you can at least diversify your money across many borrowers, and you benefit from the professional review and due diligence of the fund management team. You can also consider lending money to family members.

Investing in Mutual Funds and Exchange-Traded Funds

Mutual funds and exchange-traded funds (ETFs) rank right up there with microwave ovens, sticky notes, and cellphones as one of the best inventions. To understand their success is to grasp how and why these funds can work for you. Here are the benefits you receive when you invest in the best mutual funds and ETFs:

>> **Professional management:** Mutual funds and ETFs are managed by a portfolio manager and research team whose full-time jobs are to screen the universe of investments for those that best meet the fund's stated objectives. These professionals call and visit companies, analyze companies' financial statements, and speak with companies' suppliers and customers. In short, the team does more research and analysis than you can ever hope to do in your free time.

Fund managers are typically graduates of the top business and finance schools in the country, where they learn the principles of portfolio management and securities valuation and selection. The best fund managers typically have a decade or more of experience in analyzing and selecting investments, and many measure their experience in decades rather than years.

>> **Low fees:** The most efficiently managed stock mutual funds and ETFs cost much less than 1 percent per year in fees (bond and money-market funds cost even less). And, when you buy a *no-load fund,* you avoid paying sales commissions

(known as *loads*) on your transactions. I discuss these types of funds throughout this chapter. You can buy an ETF for a low transaction fee through the best online brokers.

>> **Diversification:** Fund investing enables you to achieve a level of diversification that's difficult to reach without tens of thousands of dollars and a lot of time to invest. If you go it alone, you should invest money in at least 15 to 20 different securities in different industries to ensure that your portfolio can withstand a downturn in one or more of the investments. Proper diversification allows a fund to receive the highest possible return at the lowest possible risk given its objectives. The most unfortunate investors during major stock market downswings have been individuals who had all their money riding on only a few stocks that plunged in price by 90 percent or more.

>> **Low cost of entry:** Most mutual funds have low minimum-investment requirements, especially for retirement account investors. (ETFs essentially have no minimum, although you don't want to do transactions involving small amounts if your brokerage firm charges a fee because that brokerage fee takes up a larger percentage of your investment amount.) Even if you have a lot of money to invest, consider funds for the low-cost, high-quality money-management services they provide.

>> **Audited performance records and expenses:** In their prospectuses, all funds are required to disclose historical data on returns, operating expenses, and other fees. The U.S. Securities and Exchange Commission (SEC) and accounting firms check these disclosures for accuracy. Also, several firms (such as Morningstar and Value Line) report hundreds of fund statistics, allowing comparisons of performance, risk, and many other factors.

>> **Flexibility in risk level:** Among the different funds, you can choose a level of risk that you're comfortable with and that meets your personal and financial goals. If you want your money to grow over a long period of time, you may want to select funds that invest more heavily in stocks. If you need current income and don't want investments that fluctuate in value as widely as stocks, you may choose more-conservative bond funds. If you want to be sure that your invested principal doesn't drop in value (perhaps because you may need your money in the short term), you can select a money-market fund.

Exploring various fund types

In this section, I discuss the major types of funds: money-market, bond, and stock funds. When fund companies develop and market funds, the names they give their funds aren't always completely accurate or comprehensive. For example, a stock fund may not be *totally* invested in stocks. Twenty percent of it may be invested in bonds. Don't assume that a fund invests exclusively in U.S. companies, either — it may invest in international firms, as well.

Money-market funds

Money-market funds are generally considered the safest type of mutual funds (although not insured or guaranteed) for people concerned about losing their invested dollars. As with bank savings accounts, the value of your original investment does not fluctuate.

When shopping for a money market fund, consider these factors:

TIP

>> **Expenses:** Within a given category of money market funds (general, Treasury, municipal, and so on), fund managers invest in the same basic securities. The market for these securities is pretty darn efficient, so "superstar" money market fund managers may eke out an extra 0.1 percent per year in yield, but not much more.

Select a money market fund that does a good job controlling its expenses. The operating expenses that the fund deducts before payment of dividends are the biggest determinant of yield. All other things being equal (which they usually are with different money market funds), lower operating expenses translate into higher yields for you.

You have no need or reason to tolerate annual operating expenses of greater than 0.5 percent. Some top-quality funds charge 0.3 percent or less annually. Remember, lower expenses don't mean that a fund company cuts corners or provides poor service. Lower expenses are possible in most cases because a fund company is successful in attracting a lot of money to invest. (Note that many money market funds have been waiving a portion of their management fee in some prior years due to ultra-low interest rates. Otherwise, the yield on their funds would have been negative.)

>> **Tax consequences:** With money market funds, all your return comes from dividends. What you actually get to keep of these returns (on non-retirement account investments) is what's left over after the federal and state governments take their cut of your investment income. If you invest money that's held outside of a retirement account and you're in a high tax bracket, you may come out ahead if you invest in tax-free money market funds. If you're in a high-tax state, then a state money market fund may be a sound move if good ones exist for your state.

REMEMBER

Tax-free refers to the taxability of the dividends that the fund pays. You don't get a tax deduction for money that you put into the fund, as you do with 401(k) or other retirement-type accounts.

>> **Location of other funds:** Consider what other investing you plan to do at the fund company where you establish a money market fund. Suppose you decide to make fund investments in stocks and bonds at T. Rowe Price. In that case, keeping a money market fund at a different firm that offers a slightly higher yield may not be worth the time and administrative hassle, especially if you don't plan on holding much cash in your money market fund.

>> **Associated services:** Good money market funds offer other useful services, such as free check writing, telephone exchange and redemptions, and automated electronic exchange services with your bank account.

Bond funds

Bond funds can make you money in the same three ways that a stock fund can: dividends, capital gains distributions, and appreciation. However, most of the time, the bulk of your return in a bond fund comes from dividends.

REMEMBER

Although an overwhelming number of bond fund choices exists (thousands, in fact), not that many remain after you eliminate high-cost funds (those with loads and high ongoing fees), low-performance funds (which are often the high-cost funds), and funds managed by fund companies and fund managers with minimal experience investing in bonds. Here are the aspects to consider when choosing bond funds:

>> **Length to maturity:** Bond fund objectives and names usually fit one of three maturity categories — short-, intermediate-, and long-term. You can earn a higher yield from investing in a bond fund that holds longer-term bonds, but as I explain in Chapter 7, such bond prices are more sensitive to changes in interest rates.

>> **Quality:** Generally speaking, the lower their issuer's credit rating, the riskier the bond. As with the risk associated with longer maturities, a fund that holds lower-quality bonds should provide higher returns for the increased risk you take. A higher yield is the bond market's way of compensating you for taking greater risk. Funds holding higher-quality bonds provide lower returns but more security.

>> **Loads and fees:** After you settle on the type of bonds you want, you must consider a bond fund's costs, including its sales commissions and annual operating fees. Stick with no-load funds that maintain lower annual operating expenses.

>> **Tax implications:** Pay attention to the taxability of the dividends that bonds pay. If you're investing in bonds inside of retirement accounts, you want taxable bonds. If you invest in bonds outside of retirement accounts, the choice between taxable versus tax-free depends on your tax bracket.

WARNING

Bond funds fluctuate in value, so invest in them only if you have sufficient money in an emergency reserve.

If you invest money for longer-term purposes, particularly retirement, you need to come up with an overall plan for allocating your money among a variety of different funds, including bond funds.

WARNING

Unfortunately, if you select bond funds based on advertised yield, you're quite likely to purchase the wrong bond funds. Bond funds and the fund companies that sell them can play more than a few games to fatten a fund's yield. Such sleights of hand make a fund's marketing and advertising departments happy because higher yields make it easier for salespeople and funds to hawk their bond funds. But remember that yield-enhancing shenanigans can leave you poorer. Here's what you need to watch out for:

>> **Lower quality:** When comparing one short-term bond fund to another, you may discover that one pays 0.5 percentage points more and decide that it looks better. However, you

may find out later that the higher-yielding fund invests 20 percent of its money in junk (non-investment-grade) bonds, whereas the other fund fully invests in high-quality bonds.

>> **Longer maturities:** Bond funds can usually increase their yield just by increasing their maturity a bit. So, if one long-term bond fund invests in bonds that mature in an average of 17 years and another fund has an average maturity of 12 years, comparing the two is a classic case of comparing apples and oranges.

>> **Giving your money back without your knowing it:** Some funds return a portion of your principal in the form of dividends. This move artificially pumps up a fund's yield but depresses its total return. When you compare bond funds, make sure you compare their total return over time (in addition to making sure the funds have comparable portfolios of bonds).

>> **Waiving of expenses:** Some bond funds, particularly newer ones, waive a portion or even all of their operating expenses to inflate the fund's yield temporarily. Yes, you can invest in a fund that waives operating fees, but you'd also buy yourself the bother of monitoring things to determine when the sale is over. Bond funds that engage in this practice often end sales quietly when the bond market is performing well. Don't forget that if you sell a bond fund (held outside of a retirement account) that has appreciated in value, you owe taxes on your profits.

Stock funds

Stock funds, as their name implies, invest in stocks. These funds are often referred to as *equity funds. Equity* — not to be confused with equity in real estate — is another word for stocks. Stock funds are often categorized by the type of stocks they primarily invest in.

Stock types are first defined by size of company (small, medium, or large). The total market value (*capitalization*) of a company's outstanding stock determines its size. Small-company stocks, for example, are usually defined as companies with total market capitalization of less than $2 billion. Mid-cap stocks are defined as having a market capitalization of between $2 and $10 billion, and large cap stocks are those with market caps over $10 billion. Stocks are further categorized as growth or value stocks:

>> **Growth stocks** represent companies that are experiencing rapidly expanding revenues and profits and typically have high stock prices relative to their current earnings or asset (book) values. These companies tend to reinvest most of their earnings in their infrastructure to fuel future expansion. Thus, growth stocks typically pay low dividends.

>> **Value stocks** are at the other end of the spectrum. Value stock investors look for good buys. They want to invest in stocks that are cheaply priced in relation to the profits per share and book value (assets less liabilities) of the company. Value stocks are usually less volatile than growth stocks.

These categories are combined in various ways to describe how a mutual fund invests its money. One fund may focus on large-company growth stocks, while another fund may limit itself to small-company value stocks. Funds are further classified by the geographical focus of their investments: U.S., international, worldwide, and so on (see the section "U.S., international, and global funds").

The best stock mutual and exchange-traded funds are excellent investment vehicles that reduce your risk, compared to purchasing individual stocks, because they

>> **Invest in dozens of stocks:** Unless you possess a lot of money to invest, you're likely to buy only a handful of stocks. If you end up with a lemon in your portfolio, it can devastate your other good choices. If such a stock represents 20 percent of your holdings, the rest of your stock selections need to increase about 25 percent in value just to get you back to even. Stock funds mitigate this risk.

For example, if a fund holds equal amounts of 50 stocks and one goes to zero, you lose only 2 percent of the fund value if the stock was an average holding. Similarly, if the fund holds 100 stocks, you lose just 1 percent. Remember that a good fund manager is more likely than you to sidestep disasters.

>> **Invest in different types of stocks:** Some funds invest in stocks of different sized companies in a variety of industries. Others may hold U.S. and international stocks. Different types of stocks generally don't move in tandem. So, if smaller-company stocks get beat up, larger-company stocks may fare better. If U.S. stocks are in the tank, international stocks may be on an upswing.

Mixing bonds and stocks: Balanced funds

Balanced funds invest in a mixture of different types of securities. Most commonly, they invest in bonds and stocks. These funds are usually less risky and volatile than funds that invest exclusively in stocks. In an economic downturn, bonds usually hold up in value better than stocks do. However, during good economic times when the stock market is booming, the bond portions of these funds tend to drag down their performance a bit.

Balanced mutual funds generally try to maintain a fairly constant percentage of investments in stocks and bonds. A similar class of funds, known as *asset allocation funds,* tends to adjust the mix of different investments according to the portfolio manager's expectations of the market. Of course, exceptions do exist — some balanced funds adjust their allocations, whereas some asset allocation funds maintain a relatively fixed mix.

REMEMBER

Most funds that shift money around instead of staying put in good investments rarely beat the market averages over a number of years.

There are also now increasing numbers of target-date or retirement-date funds, which tend to decrease their risk (and stock allocation) over time. Such funds appeal to investors who are approaching a particular future goal, such as retirement or a child's college education, and want their fund to automatically adjust as that date approaches.

TIP

Balanced funds are a way to make fund investing simple. They give you extensive diversification across a variety of investing options. They also make it easier for stock-skittish investors to invest in stocks while avoiding the high volatility of pure stock funds.

U.S., international, and global funds

Unless they have words like *international, global, worldwide,* or *world* in their names, most American-issued funds focus their investments in the United States. But even funds without one of these terms attached may invest some of their money internationally.

TIP

The only way to know for sure where a fund is currently invested (or where the fund may invest in the future) is to investigate. A fund's annual report (which can be found on the fund company's website) details where the fund is investing (the prospectus will also detail where the fund can be invested). You can also call the toll-free number of the fund company you're interested in and ask.

When a fund has the term *international* or *foreign* in its name, it typically means that the fund invests anywhere in the world *except* the United States. The term *worldwide* or *global* generally implies that a fund invests everywhere in the world, *including* the United States.

Index funds

Index funds are funds that can be (and are, for the most part) managed by a formulaic approach. An index fund's assets are invested to replicate an existing market index such as Standard & Poor's 500, an index of 500 large U.S. company stocks. (Some exchange-traded funds are index funds with the added twist that they trade on a major stock exchange.)

Over long periods (ten years or more), index funds outperform about three-quarters of their peers! How is that possible? How can mindlessly mimicking the holdings of a given index beat an intelligent, creative, MBA-endowed portfolio manager with a crack team of research analysts scouring the market for the best securities? The answer is largely cost. You can run an index fund with a much smaller management team and without spending gobs of money on research. An index fund doesn't need a team of research analysts.

In contrast to passively managed index funds, most active fund managers can't overcome the handicap of high operating expenses that pull down their funds' rates of return. As I discuss later in this chapter, operating expenses include all the fees and profit that a mutual fund extracts from a fund's returns before the returns are paid to you. For example, the average U.S. stock fund has an operating expense ratio of 1.1 percent per year. So, a U.S. stock index fund (or its peer exchange-traded fund, which is an index fund that trades on a stock exchange) with an expense ratio of just 0.1 percent per year has an advantage of 1.0 percent per year.

Another not-so-inconsequential advantage of index funds is that they can't underperform the market. Many actively managed funds do just that because of the burden of high fees and/or poor management. For money invested outside retirement accounts, index funds have an added advantage: Lower taxable capital gains distributions are made to shareholders because less trading of securities is conducted and a more stable portfolio is maintained.

Yes, index funds may seem downright boring. When you invest in them, you give up the opportunity to brag to others about your shrewd investments that beat the market averages. On the other hand, with a low-cost index fund, you have no chance of doing worse than the market (which plenty of active investment managers do).

Index funds and exchange-traded funds make sense for a portion of your investments, because beating the market is difficult for portfolio managers. The Vanguard Group (phone 800-662-7447; website www.vanguard.com), headquartered in Valley Forge, Pennsylvania, is the largest and lowest-cost provider of such funds.

Specialty (sector) funds

Specialty funds don't fit neatly into the previous categories. These funds are often known as *sector funds*, because they generally invest in securities in specific industries.

In most cases, you should avoid investing in specialty funds. Investing in stocks of a single industry defeats one of the major purposes of investing in funds — diversification. Another good reason to avoid specialty funds is that they tend to carry higher expenses than other funds.

Specialty funds that invest in real estate or precious metals may make sense for a small portion (10 percent or less) of your investment portfolio. These types of funds can help diversify your portfolio, because they can do better during times of higher inflation.

Deciphering your fund's performance

When you invest in stock funds, you can make money in three ways:

>> **Dividends:** As a fund investor, you can choose to receive your share of the dividends paid out to the fund as cash or to reinvest them in purchasing more shares in the fund. Higher-growth companies tend to pay lower dividends.

Unless you need the income to live on (if, for example, you're already retired), reinvest your dividends into buying more shares in the fund. If you reinvest outside of a retirement account, keep a record of those reinvestments because you need to factor those additional purchases into the tax calculations that you make when you sell your shares. (Most brokers will allow you to reinvest dividends paid on ETFs without a fee.)

>> **Capital gains distributions:** When a fund manager sells stocks for more than they paid, the resulting profits, known as *capital gains,* must be netted against losses and paid out to the fund's shareholders. Just as with dividends, you can reinvest your capital gains distributions in the fund.

>> **Appreciation:** The fund manager isn't going to sell all the stocks that have gone up in value. Thus, the price per share of the fund increases to reflect the gains in its stock holdings. For you, these profits are on paper until you sell the fund and lock them in. Of course, if a fund's stocks decline in value, the share price depreciates.

If you add together dividends, capital gains distributions, and appreciation, you arrive at the *total return* of a fund.

Creating your fund portfolio with asset allocation

Asset allocation simply means that you decide what percentage of your investments you place — or allocate — into bonds versus stocks and into international stocks versus U.S. stocks. (Asset allocation can also include other assets, such as small business and real estate, which are discussed in Chapters 5 and 6.)

When you invest money for the longer term, such as for retirement, you can choose among the various types of funds that I discuss in this chapter. Most people get a big headache when they try to decide how to spread their money among the choices. This section helps you begin cutting through the clutter.

Allocating for the long term

Your current age and the number of years until you retire are the biggest factors in your allocation decision. The younger you are and the more years you have before retirement, the more comfortable you should be with volatile, growth-oriented investments, such as stock funds.

Table 3-2 lists guidelines for allocating fund money that you've earmarked for long-term purposes such as retirement. You don't need an MBA or PhD to decide your asset allocation — all you need to know is how old you are and the level of risk that you desire!

TABLE 3-2 ## Asset Allocation for the Long Haul

Your Investment Attitude	Bond Fund Allocation (%)	Stock Fund Allocation (%)
Play it safe	= Age	= 100 – Age
Middle of the road	= Age – 10	= 110 – Age
Aggressive	= Age – 20	= 120 – Age

Diversifying your stock fund investments

Suppose that your investment allocation decisions suggest that you invest 50 percent in U.S. stock funds. You can choose from growth-oriented stocks and funds and those that focus on value stocks as well as from funds that focus on small-, medium-, or large-company stocks. You also need to decide what portion you want to invest in index funds (which I discuss earlier in "Index funds") versus actively managed funds that try to beat the market.

TIP

Generally, it's a good idea to diversify using different types of funds. You can diversify in one of two ways:

>> **Purchase several individual funds, each of which focuses on a different style.** For example, you can invest in a large-company value stock fund and in a small-company growth fund. I find this approach somewhat tedious. Granted, it does allow a fund manager to specialize and gain greater knowledge about a particular type of stock. But many of the best managers invest in more than one narrow range of security.

>> **Invest in a handful of funds (five to ten), each of which covers several bases and that together cover them all.** Remember, the investment delineations are somewhat arbitrary, and most funds focus on more than just one type of investment. For example, a fund may focus on small-company value stocks but may also invest in medium-company stocks. It may also invest in some that are more growth oriented.

Deciding how much you should use index versus actively managed funds is really a matter of personal taste. If you're satisfied knowing that you'll get the market rate of return and that you can't underperform the market (after accounting for your costs), index your entire portfolio. On the other hand, if you enjoy the challenge of trying to pick the better managers and want the potential to earn better than the market level of returns, don't use index funds at all. Investing in a happy medium of both, like I do, is always a safe bet.

REMEMBER

If you haven't experienced the sometimes significant plummets in stock prices that occur, you may feel queasy the next time it happens, and you've got a chunk of your nest egg in stocks. Be sure to understand the risk in stocks and what you can and can't do to reduce the volatility of your stock holdings.

Chapter **4**

Managing Risk Like a Pro

To buy and enjoy using a computer or smartphone, you don't need to know the intricacies of how each device is put together and how it works. The same holds true for investing in stocks and bonds. As a potential investor, the important thing to remember is that you can usually make more money in stocks than bonds, but stocks are generally more volatile in the short term (see Chapter 3).

In this chapter, I describe the essential strategies that seasoned investors use to manage risk. To find out more about stock market basics from a stock-issuing entity's perspective, please see the most recent edition of my book *Investing For Dummies* (Wiley).

Understanding Investment Risks

Many investors have a simplistic understanding of what risk means and how to apply it to their investment decisions. For example, when compared to the yo-yo motions of the stock market, a bank savings account may seem like a less risky place to put your money. Over the long term, however, the stock market usually beats the rate of inflation, while the interest rate on a savings account does not, especially when factoring in taxes. Thus, if you're saving your money for a long-term goal like retirement, a savings account can be a "riskier" place to put your money if you're concerned about the future purchasing power of your investments.

Before you invest, ask yourself these questions:

>> **What am I saving and investing this money for?** In other words, what's my goal?

>> **What is my timeline for this investment?** When will I likely use this money?

>> **What is the historical volatility of the investment I'm considering?** Does that suit my comfort level and timeline for this investment?

After you answer these questions, you'll have a better understanding of risk and you'll be able to match your savings goals to their most appropriate investment vehicles.

Comparing the risks of stocks and bonds

Given the relatively higher historic returns for ownership investments, some people think they should put all their money in stocks and real estate. So, what's the catch?

The risk with ownership investments is the short-term fluctuations in their value. During the last century, stocks declined, on average, by more than 10 percent once every five years. Drops in stock prices of more than 20 percent occurred, on average, once every ten years. Real-estate prices suffer similar periodic setbacks.

Therefore, in order to earn those generous long-term returns from ownership investments like stocks and real estate, you must be willing to tolerate volatility. You absolutely should not put all your money in the stock or real-estate market. Investing your emergency money or money you expect to use within the next five years in such volatile investments is not a good idea.

The shorter the time period that you have for holding your money in an investment, the less likely growth-oriented investments like stocks are to beat out lending-type investments like bonds. Table 4-1 illustrates the historical relationship between stock and bond returns based on the number of years held.

TABLE 4-1 ## Stocks versus Bonds

Number of Years Investment Held	Likelihood of Stocks Beating Bonds
1	60%
5	70%
10	80%
20	91%
30	99%

Some types of bonds have higher yields than others, but the risk-reward relationship remains intact (see Chapter 3 for more on bonds). A bond generally pays you a higher rate of interest when it has a

» **Lower credit rating:** To compensate for the higher risk of default and the higher likelihood of losing your investment

» **Longer-term maturity:** To compensate for the risk that you'll be unhappy with the bond's set interest rate if the market level of interest rates moves up

Focusing on the risks you can control

When you invest in stocks and other growth-oriented investments, you must accept the volatility of these investments. That said, you can take several actions to greatly reduce your risk when investing in these higher-potential-return investments. Invest the money that you have earmarked for the longer term in these vehicles. Minimize the risk of these investments through diversification. Don't buy just one or two stocks; buy a number of stocks. Later in this chapter, I discuss what you need to know about diversification.

Here's another risk you can control: Before you begin investing, consider paying off consumer debt. If you're paying 10-, 14-, or 18-percent interest or more on an outstanding credit card or other consumer loan, pay it off before investing. To get a comparable return through other investment vehicles (after the government takes its share of your profits), you'd have to start a new career as a loan shark. If, between federal and state taxes, you're in a 30-percent combined income tax bracket and you're paying 14-percent interest on consumer debt, you need to annually earn a whopping pre-tax return of 20 percent on your investments to justify not paying off such debt. Good luck with that!

When your only source of funds for paying off debt is a small emergency reserve equal to a few months' living expenses, paying off your debt may involve some risk. Tap into your emergency reserves only if you have a backup source — for example, the ability to borrow from a willing family member or against a retirement account balance.

Diversifying Your Investments

Diversification is one of the most powerful investment concepts. It refers to saving your eggs (or investments) in different baskets. Diversification requires you to place (or *allocate*) your money in different investments with returns that are not completely correlated, which is a fancy way of saying that when some of your investments are down in value, odds are that others are up in value.

To decrease the chances of all your investments getting clobbered at the same time, you must allocate your money in different types of investments, such as bonds, stocks, real estate, and small business. (I cover all these investments and more in Chapters 3, 5, and 6.) You can further diversify your investments by investing in domestic as well as international markets.

TIP

When one or more of the choices is an international stock fund, consider allocating a percentage of your stock fund money to overseas investments: at least 20 percent for play-it-safe investors, 25 to 35 percent for middle-of-the-road investors, and as much as 35 to 50 percent for aggressive investors.

You can look at the benefits of diversification in two ways:

» Diversification reduces the volatility in the value of your whole portfolio. In other words, your portfolio can achieve the same rate of return that a single investment can provide with less fluctuation in value.

» Diversification allows you to obtain a higher rate of return for a given level of risk.

REMEMBER

Keep in mind that no one, no matter whom they work for or what credentials they have, can guarantee returns on an investment. You can do good research and get lucky, but no one is free from the risk of losing money. Diversification allows you to hedge the risk of your investments.

Sticking with your allocations: Don't trade

Your goals and desire to take risk should drive the allocation of your investment dollars. As you get older, gradually scaling back on the riskiness (and therefore growth potential and volatility) of your portfolio generally makes sense.

Don't tinker with your portfolio daily, weekly, monthly, or even annually. (Every two to three years or so, you may want to rebalance your holdings to get your mix to a desired asset allocation, as discussed in the preceding section.) Don't engage in trading with the hopes of buying into a hot investment and selling your losers. Jumping onto a "winner" and dumping a "loser" may provide some short-term psychological comfort, but in the long term, such an investment strategy often produces below-average returns.

WARNING

When an investment gets front-page coverage and everyone is talking about its stunning rise, it's definitely time to take a reality check. The higher an investment's price rises, the greater the danger that it's overpriced. Its next move may be downward. Don't follow the herd.

Investing lump sums via dollar-cost averaging

When you have what is to you a large chunk of cash to invest — whether you received it from an accumulation of funds over the years, an inheritance, or a recent windfall from work you've done — you may have a problem deciding what to do with it. Many people, of course, would like to have your problem. (You're not complaining, right?) You want to invest your money, but you're a bit skittish — if not outright terrified — at the prospect of investing the lump of money all at once.

REMEMBER

If the money is residing in a savings or money-market account, you may feel like it's wasting away. You want to put it to work! My first words of advice are "Don't rush." Nothing is wrong with earning a small return in a money-market account. Remember that a money-market fund beats the heck out of rushing into an investment in which you may lose 20 percent or more.

TIP

Take a deep breath. You have absolutely no reason to rush into an important decision. Tell your friendly banker that when the CD matures, you want to put the proceeds into the bank's highest-yielding savings or money-market account. That way, your money continues to earn interest while you buy yourself some breathing room.

One approach to investing is called *dollar-cost averaging* (DCA). With DCA, you invest your money in equal chunks on a regular basis — such as once a month — into a diversified group of investments. For example, if you have $60,000 to invest, you can invest $2,500 per month until it's all invested, which takes a couple of years. The money awaiting future investment isn't lying fallow; you keep it in a money-market account so it can earn a bit of interest while waiting its turn.

The attraction of DCA is that it allows you to ease into riskier investments instead of jumping in all at once. If the price of the investment drops after some of your initial purchases, you can buy some later at a lower price. If you dump your entire chunk of money into an investment all at once and then it drops like a stone, you'll be kicking yourself for not waiting.

The flip side of DCA is that when your investment of choice appreciates in value, you may wish that you had invested your money faster. Another drawback of DCA is that you may get cold feet as you continue to pour money into an investment that's dropping in value.

DCA can also cause headaches with your taxes when the time comes to sell investments held outside retirement accounts. When you buy an investment at many different times and prices, the accounting becomes muddied as you sell blocks of the investment.

TIP

DCA is most valuable when the money you want to invest represents a large portion of your total assets and you can stick to a schedule. Make DCA automatic so you're less likely to abandon plans if the investment falls after your initial purchases.

Buying and Selling Stocks

Stocks are intended to be long-term holdings. When you buy stocks, you should plan to hold them for at least five years or more — and preferably seven to ten. When stocks suffer a setback, it may take months or even years for them to come back. Over long periods of time, based on historic performance, you can expect to earn an average of about 9 percent per year total return by investing in stocks.

When you invest in stocks, many (perhaps too many) choices exist. Besides the tens of thousands of stocks from which you can select, you also can invest in mutual funds, exchange-traded funds (ETFs), or hedge funds, or you can have a stockbroker select for you.

You invest in stocks to share in the rewards of capitalistic economies. When you invest in stocks, you do so through the stock market.

Defining "The Market"

When people talk about "The Market," they're usually referring to the U.S. stock market. Even more specifically, they're usually speaking about the *Dow Jones Industrial Average*, created by Charles Dow and Eddie Jones, which is a widely watched index or measure of the performance of the U.S. stock market. Dow and Jones, two reporters in their 30s, started publishing a paper that you may have heard of — the *Wall Street Journal* — in 1889. Like the modern-day version, the 19th-century *Wall Street Journal* reported current financial news. Dow and Jones also compiled stock prices of larger, important companies and created and calculated indexes to track the performance of the U.S. stock market.

The Dow Jones Industrial Average ("the Dow") market index tracks the performance of 30 large companies that are headquartered in the United States. The Dow 30 includes such companies as telecommunications giant Verizon Communications; airplane manufacturer Boeing; beverage maker Coca-Cola; energy giant Chevron; technology behemoths Apple, IBM, Intel, and Microsoft; drug makers Amgen and Merck; fast-food king McDonald's; and retailers Home Depot and Walmart.

Looking at major stock market indexes

Just as New York City isn't the only city to visit or live in, the 30 stocks in the Dow Jones Industrial Average are far from representative of all the different types of stocks that you can invest in. Here are some other important market indexes and the types of stocks they track:

>> **Standard & Poor's (S&P) 500:** Similar to the types of stocks in the Dow Jones Industrial Average, the S&P 500 tracks the price of 500 larger-company U.S. stocks. These 500 big companies account for about 80 percent of the total market value of the tens of thousands of stocks traded in the United States. Thus, the S&P 500 is a much broader and more representative index of the larger-company stocks in the United States than the Dow Jones Industrial Average is.

>> **Russell 2000:** This index tracks the market value of 2,000 smaller U.S. company stocks of various industries. Although small-company stocks tend to move in tandem with larger-company stocks over the longer term, it's not unusual for one to rise or fall more than the other or for one index to fall while the other rises in a given year. For example, in 2001, the Russell 2000 actually rose 2.5 percent while the S&P 500 fell 11.9 percent. In 2007, the Russell 2000 lost 1.6 percent versus a gain of 5.5 percent for the S&P 500. Be aware that smaller-company stocks tend to be more volatile.

>> **Wilshire 5000:** Despite its name, the Wilshire 5000 index actually tracks the prices of just 3,400 stocks of U.S. companies of all sizes — small, medium, and large. Many consider this index, which was originally named for the number of stocks in it, the broadest and most representative of the overall U.S. stock market.

>> **Nasdaq Index:** This index, which tracks stocks listed on the Nasdaq exchange, is heavily tilted toward technology companies. This index includes stocks in other industry groups but is not nearly as diversified in terms of industry representation as the S&P 500. While it does include companies of varying sizes, the biggest 100 companies (known as the Nasdaq 100) make up the vast majority of the market value of the index. This includes many companies you've likely heard of, including Microsoft, Apple, Amazon, Alphabet (formerly Google), Facebook, Intel, Cisco Systems,

PepsiCo, Comcast, Netflix, NVIDIA, Adobe, Costco, PayPal, Amgen, Texas Instruments, Charter Communications, Broadcom, Tesla, Gilead Sciences, and Starbucks.

>> **MSCI EAFE:** Stocks don't exist only in the United States. MSCI's EAFE index tracks the prices of stocks in the other major developed countries of the world. *EAFE* stands for Europe, Australasia, and Far East.

>> **MSCI Emerging Markets:** This index follows the value of stocks in the less economically developed but "emerging" countries, such as Brazil, China, Russia, Taiwan, India, South Korea, Chile, Mexico, and so on. These stock markets tend to be more volatile than those in established economies.

TIP

You often hear references to bull markets and bear markets when folks discuss the stock market. A *bull market* means a good market for investors, and a *bear market* means a bad market for investors.

Counting reasons to use indexes

Indexes serve several purposes. First, they can quickly give you an idea of how particular types of stocks perform compared to other types of stocks. Indexes also allow you to compare or benchmark the performance of your stock market investments. If you invest primarily in large-company U.S. stocks, for example, you should compare the overall return of the stocks in your portfolio to a comparable index, such as the S&P 500.

You may also hear about some other types of more narrowly focused indexes, including those that track the performance of stocks in particular industries, such as banking, pharmaceuticals, restaurants, semiconductors, software, textiles, and utilities. Other indexes cover the stock markets of other countries, such as the United Kingdom, Germany, South Korea, Canada, and Hong Kong.

WARNING

Focusing your investments in the stocks of just one or two industries or smaller countries is dangerous due to the lack of diversification and your lack of expertise in making the difficult decision about what to invest in and when. It's not enough to know that a particular sector is growing fast because that doesn't necessarily translate into future stock appreciation for those companies. The sector might be greatly overpriced right now or about to fall on tough times. Thus, I highly recommend that you ignore these narrower indexes. Many companies, largely out of desire for publicity, develop their own indexes. If the news media report on these indexes, the index developer obtains free advertising.

Buying stocks via mutual funds and exchange-traded funds

If you're busy and suffer no delusions about your expertise, you'll love the best stock mutual funds. Investing in stocks through mutual funds can be as simple as dialing a toll-free phone number or logging on to a fund company's website, completing application forms, and zapping them some money.

Mutual funds take money invested by people like you and me and pool it in a single investment portfolio in securities, such as stocks and bonds. The portfolio is then professionally managed. Stock mutual funds, as the name suggests, invest primarily or exclusively in stocks (some stock funds sometimes invest a bit in other stuff, such as bonds).

Exchange-traded funds (ETFs) are in many ways similar to mutual funds, specifically index funds (see Chapter 3), except that they trade on a stock exchange. One potential attraction is that some ETFs offer investors the potential for even lower operating expenses than comparable mutual funds and may be tax-friendlier.

Stock funds include many advantages:

REMEMBER

>> **Diversification:** Buying individual stocks on your own is relatively time-consuming and costly unless you buy reasonable chunks (100 shares or so) of each stock. But to buy 100 shares each in, say, a dozen companies' stocks to ensure diversification, you need about $60,000 if the stocks that you buy average $50 per share.

>> **Professional management:** Even if you have big bucks to invest, funds offer something that you can't deliver: professional, full-time management. Fund managers peruse a company's financial statements and otherwise track and analyze its business strategy and market position. The best managers put in long hours and possess lots of expertise and experience in the field. (If you've been misled into

believing that with minimal effort, you can rack up market-beating returns by selecting your own stocks, please be sure to read the rest of this chapter.)

Look at it this way: Funds are a huge time-saver. On your next day off, would you rather sit in front of your computer and research semiconductors and paper manufacturers, or would you rather enjoy dinner or a movie with family and friends? (The answer to that question depends on who your family and friends are!)

>> **Low costs — if you pick 'em right:** To convince you that funds aren't a good way for you to invest, those with a vested interest, such as stock-picking newsletter pundits, may point out the high fees that some funds charge. An element of truth rings here: Some funds are expensive, charging you a couple percent or more per year in operating expenses on top of hefty sales commissions.

But just as you wouldn't want to invest in a fund that a novice with no track record manages, why would you want to invest in a high-cost fund? Contrary to the "You get what you pay for" notion often trumpeted by those trying to sell you something at an inflated price, some of the best managers are the cheapest to hire. Through a *no-load* (commission-free) mutual fund, you can hire a professional, full-time money manager to invest $10,000 for a mere $20 to $100 per year. Some index funds and exchange-traded funds charge even less.

As with all investments, funds have some drawbacks. Consider the following:

>> **The issue of control is a problem for some investors.** If you like feeling in control, sending your investment dollars to a seemingly black-box process where others decide when and in what to invest your money may unnerve you. However, you need to be more concerned about the potential blunders that you may make investing in individual stocks of your own choosing or, even worse, those stocks pitched to you by a broker. And the financial markets can change fast, challenge your recent thinking, stress you out, and quickly make you feel like you're actually not in control!

> **» Taxes are a concern when you invest in funds outside of retirement accounts.** Because the fund manager decides when to sell specific stock holdings, some funds may produce more taxable distributions. That doesn't rule out investing in funds, however, as there are some really good tax-friendly funds.

Using hedge funds and privately managed funds

Like mutual funds, *hedge funds* are a managed investment vehicle. In other words, an investment management team researches and manages the fund's portfolio. However, hedge funds are oriented to affluent investors and typically charge steep fees — a 1.0 to 1.5 percent annual management fee plus a 15 to 20 percent cut of the annual fund returns.

No proof exists that hedge funds as a group perform better than mutual funds. In fact, the objective studies that I've reviewed show inferior hedge fund returns, which makes sense. Those high hedge fund fees depress their returns. Notwithstanding the small number of hedge funds that have produced better long-term returns, too many affluent folks invest in hedge funds due to the fund's hyped marketing and the badge of exclusivity they offer.

WARNING

Please be aware that there is a surplus of various hedge/private investment managers, most of whom are small players in the investment management world, writing blogs, preening on social media, and serving as "experts" and "gurus" in other media who make all sorts of unsubstantiated and unverified claims. The common thread of such claims, as you may guess, is how awesome these folks are in supposedly having seen what was coming in the financial markets and supposedly positioning their clients' investment holdings well, leading to the production of high returns. This fibbing is enabled by the fact that private money managers and hedge fund managers don't have public performance data requirements.

Selecting individual stocks yourself

More than a few investing gurus and books suggest and enthusiastically encourage people to do their own stock picking. However, the vast majority of investors are better off *not* picking their own stocks, in my observations and experience.

I've long been an advocate of educating yourself and taking responsibility for your own financial affairs, but taking responsibility for your finances doesn't mean you should do *everything* yourself. Table 4-2 includes some thoughts to consider about choosing your own stocks.

TABLE 4-2 **Why You're Buying Your Own Stocks**

Good Reasons to Pick Your Own Stocks	Bad Reasons to Pick Your Own Stocks
You enjoy the challenge.	You think you can beat the best money managers. (If you can, you're probably in the wrong profession!)
You want to learn more about business.	You want more control over your investments, which you think may happen if you understand the companies that you invest in.
You possess a substantial amount of money to invest.	You think that mutual funds are for people who aren't smart enough to choose their own stocks.
You're a buy-and-hold investor.	You're attracted to the ability to trade your stocks anytime you want.

Some popular investing blogs, websites, and books try to convince investors that they can do a *better* job than the professionals at picking their own stocks. Amateur investors, however, need to devote a lot of study to become proficient at stock selection. Many professional investors work 60+ hours a week at investing, but you're unlikely to be willing to spend that much time on it. Don't let the popularity of those do-it-yourself stock-picking online gurus and books lead you astray.

REMEMBER

Choosing a stock isn't as simple as visiting a restaurant chain (or buying a pair of shoes or an iGadget), liking it, buying its stock, and then sitting back and getting rich watching your stock zoom to the moon. I've had investing ideas myself for picking individual stocks, and if I had acted on them, I would have done very well in some cases and terribly in others. Thanks to the decades of my adult life and observing the financial markets, I know that stock picking is much harder than most people think it is.

If you invest in stocks, I think you know by now that guarantees don't exist. But as in many of life's endeavors, you can buy individual stocks in good and not-so-good ways. So, if you want to select your own individual stocks, check out the most recent edition of my book *Investing For Dummies* (Wiley), where I explain how to best research and trade them.

Spotting the right times to buy and sell

After you know about the different types of stock markets and ways to invest in stocks, you may wonder how you can build wealth with stocks and not lose your shirt. Nobody wants to buy stocks before a big drop.

The stock market is reasonably efficient. A company's stock price normally reflects many smart people's assessments as to what is a fair price. Thus, it's not realistic for an investor to expect to discover a system for how to "buy low and sell high." Some professional investors may be able to spot good times to buy and sell particular stocks, but consistently doing so is enormously difficult.

TIP

The simplest and best way to make money in the stock market is to consistently and regularly feed new money into building a diversified and larger portfolio. If the market drops, you can use your new investment dollars to buy more shares. The danger of trying to time the market is that you may be "out" of the market when it appreciates greatly and "in" the market when it unexpectedly plummets.

REMEMBER

When bad news and pessimism abound and the stock market has dropped, it's actually a much safer and better time to buy stocks. You may even consider shifting some of your money out of your safer investments, such as bonds, and invest more aggressively in stocks. Investors feel during these times that prices can drop further, but if you buy and hold for the long term, you'll be amply rewarded.

Avoiding problematic stock-buying practices

You may be curious about ways to buy individual stocks, but note that if the methods you're curious about appear in the following list, it's because I *don't* recommend using them. You can greatly increase your chances of success and earn higher returns if you avoid these commonly made stock-investing mistakes:

>> **Beware of broker conflicts of interest:** Some investors make the mistake of investing in individual stocks through a broker who earns commissions. The standard pitch from these firms and their brokers is that they maintain research departments that monitor and report on stocks. Their brokers, using this research, tell you when and what to buy, sell, or hold. Sounds good in theory, but this system has significant problems.

WARNING

Many brokerage firms happen to be in another business that creates enormous conflicts of interest in producing objective company reviews. These investment firms also solicit companies to help them sell new stock and bond issues. To gain this business, the brokerage firms need to demonstrate enthusiasm and optimism for the company's future prospects.

Brokerage analysts who, with the best of intentions, write negative reports about a company find their careers hindered in a variety of ways. Some firms fire such analysts. Companies that the analysts criticize exclude those analysts from analyst meetings about the company. So, most analysts who know what's good for their careers and their brokerage firms don't write disapproving reports (but some do take chances).

>> **Don't short-term trade or try to time the market:** Unfortunately (for themselves), some investors track their stock investments closely and believe they need to sell after short holding periods — months, weeks, or even days. With the growth of internet and computerized trading, such shortsightedness has taken a turn for the worse as more investors now engage in a foolish process known as *day trading,* where they buy and sell a stock within the same day!

REMEMBER

Stocks are intended to be long-term holdings. You shouldn't buy stocks if you don't plan to hold them for at least five years or more — and preferably seven to ten. When stocks suffer a setback, it may take months or even years for them to come back.

>> **Be wary of gurus:** It's tempting to want to consult a guru who claims to be able to foresee an impending major decline and get you out of an investment before it tanks. Believe me when I say that plenty of these pundits are talking up such supposed prowess. The financial crisis of 2008 brought an avalanche of prognosticators out of the woodwork claiming that if you had been listening to them, you could not only have side-stepped losses but also made money.

WARNING

From having researched many such claims (see the "Guru Watch" section of my website, www.erictyson.com), I can tell you that nearly all these folks significantly misrepresented their past predictions and recommendations. And the few who made some halfway decent predictions in the recent short term had poor or unremarkable longer-term track records.

>> **Shun penny stocks:** Thousands of smaller-company stocks trade on the over-the-counter *penny stocks* market. Some of these companies are quite small and sport low prices per share that range from pennies to several dollars, hence the name *penny stocks.*

The biggest problem with buying penny stocks is that some are grossly overpriced, often due to dishonest practices by individual brokers or brokerage firms. Just as you don't make good investment returns by purchasing jewelry that's marked up 100 percent, you don't have a fighting chance to make decent money on penny stocks that the broker may flog with similar markups.

Proven investment strategies

TIP

To maximize your chances of stock market investment success, do the following:

>> **Don't try to time the markets.** Anticipating where the stock market and specific stocks are heading is next to impossible, especially over the short term. Economic factors, which are influenced by thousands of elements, as well as human emotions, determine stock market prices. Be a regular buyer of stocks with new savings. As I discuss earlier in this chapter, consider buying more stocks when they're on sale and market pessimism is running high. Don't make the mistake of bailing out when the market is down!

>> **Diversify your investments.** Invest in the stocks of different-sized companies in varying industries around the world. When assessing your investments' performance, examine your whole portfolio at least once a year, and calculate your total return after expenses and trading fees.

>> **Keep trading costs, management fees, and commissions to a minimum.** These costs represent a big drain on your returns. If you invest through an individual broker or a financial advisor who earns a living on commissions, odds are that you're paying more than you need to be. And you're likely receiving biased advice, too.

>> **Pay attention to taxes.** Like commissions and fees, federal and state taxes are a major investment "expense" that you can minimize. Contribute most of your money to your tax-advantaged retirement accounts. You can invest your money outside of retirement accounts, but keep an eye on taxes. Calculate your annual returns on an *after*-tax basis.

>> **Don't overestimate your ability to pick the big-winning stocks.** One of the best ways to invest in stocks is through mutual funds and exchange-traded funds, which allow you to use an experienced, full-time money manager at a low cost to perform all the investing grunt work for you.

Chapter **5**

Investing in a Small Business

Many Americans have found that investing in small business is an effective way to build wealth. The lingo of the business world — cash flow, profit and loss statements, accounts receivable, debt-to-equity ratio, and so on — makes small-business ownership appear far more complicated than it really is. Don't be fooled. You're probably more acquainted with the basic concepts of doing business than you think. In this chapter, I cover some essential considerations when choosing to start, own, or buy a small business.

Owning a Small Business

A *small-business owner* (or entrepreneur), in my estimation, is anyone who owns a business that has 100 or fewer employees, period. Everyone who hangs out a shingle qualifies for the title no matter whether the business is private, public, barely surviving, or soaring off the charts.

You're a small-business owner whether you've been in the saddle one day, one week, or one decade; whether you're male or female and have a college degree or not; whether you work out of your home or on a fishing boat somewhere off the coast of Alaska.

Being a small-business owner doesn't mean that you must work 70 hours a week, make a six-figure income, or offer a unique product or service. Many successful small-business owners work at their craft 40 hours a week or less and some work part-time at their business in addition to holding a regular job. The clear majority of small-business owners I know provide products or services quite similar to what's already in the marketplace and make reasonable but not extraordinary sums of money — and, thanks largely to the independence that small-business owner-ship offers, are perfectly happy doing so!

The reasons to own

There are many reasons to give your boss the heave-ho. This section, though, sticks with the best reasons for choosing to own a business:

>> **The satisfaction of creation:** Have you ever experienced the pride of building a chair, preparing a gourmet meal, or completing a home repair? Or how about providing a needed counseling service that helps people solve their vexing financial problems? The small-business owner gets to experience the thrill of creation daily, not to mention the satisfaction of solving a customer's problem.

>> **Establishment of their own culture:** No more standing around the water cooler complaining about "the way things are around here." After you start your own business, the way things are around here is a direct function of the way you intend them to be.

>> **Financial upside:** Consider Daymond John and Lori Greiner (entrepreneurs and *Shark Tank* investors). It's no surprise that these one-time small-business owners are among the nation's wealthiest individuals. (A recent Small Business Administration study concluded definitively that although small-business ownership is risky, small-business owners had a significantly higher probability of being classified as high income and high wealth than their employed counterparts.)

>> **Self-sufficiency:** For many people, working for someone else has proven to be a less-than-gratifying experience. As a

result of such unfulfilling experiences, some people have discovered that if they want to provide for themselves and their families, they'd better create the opportunity themselves. It's either that or be willing to occasionally spend a long wait in the unemployment line.

>> **Flexibility:** Perhaps you prefer to work in the evenings because that's when your spouse works, or you want to spend more time with the kids during the day. Or you may prefer taking frequent three-day-weekend jaunts rather than a few full-week vacations every year. As a small-business owner, despite the long hours you work, you should have more control over your schedule. After all, you're the boss, and you can usually tailor your schedule to meet your personal needs, as well as those of your customers.

>> **Special perks:** Small-business owners have several advantages over the typical employee. For example, small-business owners can sock away tens of thousands of dollars into their retirement accounts per year free of federal and state income taxes. And yes, similar to those corporate execs who enjoy various other tax deductions, small-business owners also have the option of writing off such costs as long as they adhere to IRS rules.

The reasons not to own

Considering the resounding potential benefits, why would any reasonable soul elect to continue receiving a paycheck? Why wouldn't everyone want to own a business? Let us count the nays:

>> **Responsibility:** When you're a small-business owner, not only does your family depend on your business success, but so do your partners, your employees and their families, your customers, and sometimes your vendors. As much as they love their small businesses, every now and then even the most enthusiastic small-business owners wax nostalgic for the good old days when they would leisurely walk out the door — really, truly done for the day.

If you're the type of person who sometimes takes on more responsibility than you can handle and works too many hours, beware that another drawback of running your own business is that you may be prone to becoming a workaholic.

WARNING

>> **Competition:** Although some people thrive on competition, that same competition comes back to haunt you by threatening your security. You soon find out that a host of hungry competitors is pursuing your customers and threatening your livelihood, whether by cutting prices or offering a more complete package of unique services. Sure, competition is what makes capitalism go 'round, but you need to remember that when you have a competition, someone wins and someone loses. That loser can be you.

>> **Change:** Products and services come, and products and services go. Nothing is sacred in the business of doing business, and the pace of change today is significantly faster than it was a generation ago — and it shows no signs of slowing down. If you don't enjoy change and the commotion it causes, then perhaps the stability that a larger, more bureaucratic organization provides is best for you.

>> **Chance:** Interest rates, the economy, theft, fire, natural disasters, sickness, pestilence — the list goes on. Any of these random events can send your business reeling.

>> **Red tape:** Taxes, healthcare reform, bureaucracy, tariffs, duties, treaties, OSHA, FDA, government-mandated shutdowns, glurg, glurg, glurg.

>> **Business failure:** Finally, as if this list of small-business enemies isn't long enough, the owner faces the specter of the ultimate downside: business failure in the form of bankruptcy. This is the stage where the owner stands back and watches the creditors swoop in like vultures to devour their remaining business — and sometimes personal — assets.

Now, contrast the small-business owner's failure to that of *Fortune* 500 employees who fail, collect a tidy severance check as they pack up their belongings, and wave goodbye on their way to register for unemployment compensation. No life's savings lost for these people, no second mortgages hanging over their home, no asterisks on the credit report. In my opinion, no other failure in the business world is as painful as the one facing the small-business owner. More than any other reason, this extreme cost of failure is the primary reason that owning a small business isn't for everyone.

Starting Your Own Small Business

In theory, all businesses have three ownership options:

>> Privately held, with the founder being the only shareholder

>> Privately held, with the founder sharing ownership with partners and/or other shareholders

>> Publicly held, with the founder sharing ownership with the general public via one of the public stock markets

In reality, of course, most businesses have only the first two options — going it alone or having partners or minority shareholders. Few businesses have the management, resources, and appeal needed to go public, either at the start-up stage or during the business's growth.

REMEMBER

There's no right or wrong answer as to which of the three options you should use, but there is a right or wrong way to determine which one works best for you. At the heart of making that decision is — you guessed it — you! You're the primary ingredient that will determine which of the three options is best for your business. The criteria you need to use in making this decision include the kind of person you are, the way you communicate, the way you delegate, and the way you work with people.

The kind of business you intend to start can also be a factor. If, for example, you intend to start a high-tech manufacturing business, you may find that the key employees you want to hire will demand some ownership (such as stock options) as part of their compensation packages. On the other hand, if you intend to go into the consulting business, sole ownership is the likely ticket for you.

The following sections offer a brief discussion of the pros and cons of each of the three ownership options.

You as the sole owner

Being the only owner has the following advantages:

>> **It's generally easier, quicker, and less expensive.** You don't need any lawyers to write up a Partnership Agreement or assist in determining answers to all the questions that a Partnership Agreement requires.

>> **The profits belong solely to you.** You don't have to share the fruits of your hard work.

>> **You have no need for consensus.** Your way is the only way.

>> **You don't waste time catering to the often-aggravating demands of shareholders, minority or otherwise.** There's no possibility of shareholder lawsuits.

On the other hand, being the only owner has the following disadvantages:

>> **You have no one to share the risk with.** This is the downside of the "profits belong solely to you" advantage described in the preceding list.

>> **Your limited skills have to carry your business until you can hire someone with complementary skills.** The small-business owner has to wear many hats; unfortunately, many of those hats simply don't fit. The day you can begin hiring employees who are capable in areas where you're not will be one of the highlights of your small-business career.

>> **Single ownership can be lonely.** Many times, you'll wish you had someone with whom you could share the problems and stress. If you're lucky, you may be able to do this with trusted senior employees. Of course, if you have good friends and/or a strong marriage partner, these people can also be a source of much-needed support.

Sharing ownership

Partners make sense when they can bring needed capital, along with complementary small-business management skills, to your company. Unfortunately, partners also present the opportunity for turmoil, and especially in the early stages of a business's growth, turmoil takes time, burns energy, and costs money — all of which most small-business founders lack.

If you're one of those rare individuals who is fortunate enough to have found the right partner, go for it; work out a deal. It has been proven many times over: A partnership in the right hands can outperform a sole proprietorship in the right hands.

Having *minority shareholders* (any and all shareholders who collectively own less than 50 percent) can also make sense, especially after the business is out of the blocks and has accumulated value. The most common methods of putting stock in the hands of employees include stock-option plans, bonuses, and Employee Stock Ownership Plans (ESOPs).

WARNING

Minority shareholders can be a pain; they have legal rights that often run counter to the wishes of the majority. Because majority shareholders are ceded the right to make the final decisions, courts have determined that minority shareholders must have an avenue of appeal. Thus, minority shareholders, particularly in today's litigious society, sometimes look to the courts whenever they feel their rights of ownership are being violated.

REMEMBER

Because of the potentially tenuous relationship that can exist between majority and minority shareholders, you should always — I repeat, *always!* — involve an attorney when inviting minority shareholders to the party, and you should always include a buy-sell agreement in the deal. If the relationship doesn't turn out to be what all parties expected, buy-sell agreements establish procedures for issuing, valuing, and selling shares of the company, including how to determine the value of shares when one or more of the owners want to cash out.

Occasionally, especially where venture capital financing is involved, the founder of the business may find themself working for majority shareholders. Fortunately, this situation rarely occurs because the typical small-business founder has already proven that taking orders from others is not exactly one of their inherent strengths. On the infrequent occasions when this situation does occur, often the founder of the company is the first one to get the boot when the going gets tough, as the chief financiers step in to protect their investment. That's why I strongly recommend that you find a way to retain majority control.

Deciding between sole and shared ownership

Still confused as to whether you want to go it alone or share ownership? Answer the following questions to help you make the decision:

>> **Do you believe that you need a partner?** Do you absolutely, positively need a partner? To provide cash? Knowledge? If you do, that settles the issue; if you don't, continue with the following questions.

Providing cash and additional knowledge are correct reasons for choosing a partner. Incorrect reasons include picking a partner because they're your friend or picking a partner because you're afraid of running a business by yourself.

>> **Are you capable of working with partners or shareholders?** Will you have a problem sharing the decisions and the profits as well as the risks?

>> **Does your business fit the multiple-ownership profile?** In other words, does your business have room for two partners, and is it a business that has the growth potential to support two partners? Will a partner have an important role in the organization? Would your partner's complementary skills enhance the business's chance for success?

>> **What are the legal requirements of multiple ownership?** Can you live within these legal parameters? (Consult with an attorney if you have questions.)

>> **What do you have in common with other business owners who have opted for multiple ownership? Where do you see conflicts?** Ask your banker, accountant, or attorney for the names of other business owners who have opted for multiple ownership. Interview those owners and get their feedback on the list of pluses and minuses.

>> **What's the likelihood of finding a partner with complementary skills and a personality compatible with yours?** This depends on how wired into the business community you are and what line of work you're going into. If you have a lot of business contacts and know exactly what you want, finding a partner may be easy. More typically, it isn't.

After you answer these questions, you should have enough information to make the partners-or-not decision, but take your time. Make a list of pros and cons and try to answer this question: Will your business have a better chance of success with just you at the helm, or are a potential partner's skills immediately needed?

If you opt for multiple or shared ownership, you'll have to live with the decision for a long, long time. If you elect sole ownership at the start, however, you can always seek partners later if you feel that you need them to achieve the business success that you desire.

Going public: Cashing in

No question about it, the lure of liquidity and the possibility of interest-free capital can be overpowering to the small-business owner, especially after years of personally guaranteeing debt, scraping for money, and living on a reduced (or sometimes no) salary. Many small-business owners at one time or another fantasize about going public, yet few businesses ever make it. The biggest reason why so few small businesses go public is that the stock markets are selective; they function for businesses that have outstanding track records and that meet particular hurdles. (Although this statement may be a bit hard to swallow if you've personally lost money investing in newly issued stock that went belly up, it still generally holds true.)

WARNING

In truth, going public has downsides that are easily overlooked. Although the capital raised may be interest-free, it is by no means hassle-free. The army of outside shareholders that comes with going public, in concert with the Securities and Exchange Commission (SEC), requires an avalanche of public filings. Yes, a public business is liquid, but at what cost to management's time? You also have to pay hefty fees to investment bankers to issue stock and to the stock exchange to initiate your listing and to maintain it over time. And in public companies, every shareholder, customer, media person, and competitor can peer into your financial records and ask you those questions that you may not have the time or the desire to answer.

Determining your start-up cash needs

Before you determine where you're going to get your start-up funds, you need to understand that your business's initial cash requirements include not only one-time start-up costs but also working capital and a reserve. Here's what these requirements mean:

>> **One-time start-up costs:** *Start-up costs* include such one-time expenses as legal fees, licenses and permits, utility and lease deposits, furniture and fixtures, inventory, leasehold improvements (such as remodels or additions to the store or office space you rent or lease), signage, and everything you need to initially open for business. Consult another business's profit and loss statement (P&L) or a pro forma P&L sample on a business plan template for a listing

of the typical day-to-day ongoing expenses you're going to incur.

>> **Working capital:** *Working capital* is the cash you need to stay open for business. It includes such ongoing, everyday expenditures as inventory and raw materials, accounts receivable, hiring of employees, and the general day-to-day operation of your business until you become consistently profitable and can fund the cost of operations out of internally generated cash flow. Don't forget to include debt repayments — both interest and principal — when arriving at this figure. (Although principal payments aren't an expense, they do reduce available capital.)

>> **Reserve:** The *reserve* is the amount of capital you need to overcome forecasting mistakes and/or make up for variances from your budget. If you end up having neither forecasting mistakes nor budget variances, I suggest you give Guinness World Records a call!

So, where's all this money going to come from? You can use two basic methods to finance your start-up:

>> **Bootstrapping:** The internal generation of initial financing, using primarily your own personal resources, sometimes complemented by various forms of equity investments or loans from family and friends.

>> **Outsourcing:** The external generation of financing for both start-up expenses and ongoing business needs, using outside resources, such as banks, angel investors, venture capitalists, and crowdfunding.

For most start-ups, bootstrapping is a much more likely source of funds than outsourcing. Besides, providers of outsourced funds aren't likely to give you the money you need unless they see that you've done your bootstrapping first.

Whether you bootstrap the financing of your business or finance it by using money from outsiders, you must first estimate your cash needs. Why? If you plan to go the bootstrapping route, you need to estimate your cash needs to minimize the chances of running out of money, a situation that can lead to the failure of your business and the loss of all the invested capital.

If you plan to outsource your capital, you need to estimate your cash needs to assure potential lenders that you have solid projections for your future cash needs.

WARNING

Just as remodeling work on a home almost always takes longer and costs more than expected, many entrepreneurs find that their start-up requires more cash than they originally expected. That's why you must allow yourself sufficient time to investigate, reflect on, and estimate the costs associated with starting your chosen business. If you end up obtaining outside capital, nothing shouts inexperience like having to go back to your source at a later date and ask for more money. Bankers and investors don't like oversights and mistakes, especially when those mistakes have to do with their money.

Buying an Existing Business

Successfully running the business day in and day out is much harder for most people than finding and buying it. Some succeed wildly at running the business they buy; others fail miserably. So what, then, are the traits common to people who successfully buy and operate an existing small business? The following sections cover them.

REMEMBER

Above all else, being persistent, patient, and willing to spend time on things that don't lead to immediate results pays off. You need to be willing to sort through the rubbish to find the keepers. If you're a person who needs immediate gratification in terms of completing a deal, you may become miserable as you search, or you may end up rushing into a bad deal. Try breaking the process into steps to provide more success points and give yourself time for clear thinking.

Understanding why to buy a business

Here are some reasons why you may want to buy an existing business rather than build one from scratch:

>> **To reduce start-up hassles and headaches:** Running a business is always a juggling act, but you often have more balls in the air during those start-up years than at any other time in the life of the business. Beyond formulating a

business plan, you have to develop a marketing plan, find customers, hire employees, locate space, and possibly incorporate. Although you still need a game plan when buying an existing business, many of these start-up tasks have already been done.

>> **To lessen your risk:** In situations where a business has an operating history and offers a product or service with a demonstrated market, you remove some of the risk when you buy an existing company (compared with starting from scratch). Although no investment is a sure thing, the risk involved in an already-established business should be significantly lower than the risk involved in a start-up.

>> **To increase profits by adding value:** Finding a business that has the potential to improve operating efficiency and expand into new markets is difficult but not impossible — if you have the time and patience to wait for the right one to come along. In fact, finding small companies that are undervalued relative to the potential they have to offer is probably easier to do than finding undervalued stocks or real estate when investing in those markets.

>> **To establish cash flow:** One of the biggest unknowns involved in starting a business from scratch is estimating the new business's cash flow, otherwise known for sale or acquisition purposes as EBITDA (Earnings Before Interest, Taxes, Depreciation and Amortization.) When you buy an existing business, the track record of the previous owners has already answered most questions pertaining to cash flow. Assuming that you don't walk in and make immediate, glaring changes to the business's products or operations, the cash flow pattern should continue somewhat as it has done in the past.

>> **To capitalize on someone else's good idea:** You don't need an original idea to go into business for yourself. Plenty of successful small-business people enjoy running a business; whether they repair cars or trim trees doesn't matter. If you know you want to own a business but you lack an idea for a product or service to sell, chalk up another good reason to buy an existing business. Just make sure that you have some passion and expertise for the industry you're thinking about joining.

>> **To open locked doors:** In certain businesses, you can enter geographic territories only as a result of buying an existing business. For example, suppose that you want to own a Lexus dealership within an hour of where you currently live. If Lexus isn't granting any more new dealerships, your only ticket into the automobile industry may be to buy an existing Lexus dealership in your area.

>> **To inherit an established customer base:** If you're not good at selling (maybe because you dislike it), buying a business may be the best way for you to enter the world of business ownership. After all, buying an existing business gives you a ready-built stable of customers, which means you don't have to recruit them yourself. Then, if you can provide quality products or services and meet customers' needs, you can see your business grow through word-of-mouth referrals.

Knowing when you shouldn't buy

Of course, you can find more than a few downsides to buying an existing business. Similar to the advantages, the relative weight of these disadvantages depends largely on your personality and available resources.

>> **You dislike inherited baggage:** When you buy an existing business, you get the bad along with the good. All businesses have their share of problems and issues. Do you have the disposition and ability to motivate your employees to change or to fire employees who don't want to change? Do you have the patience to work at improving the company's products and reputation? Do you have the cash to upgrade the technology or remodel the dated offices? All these issues are barriers to running and adding value to a company. Think back on your other work experiences for clues about what challenges you've tackled and how you felt about them.

>> **You're going to skimp on inspections:** If you think buying a company is easy, think again. Before you sign on the dotted line, you should know exactly what you're buying, so you need to do a comprehensive inspection (also known as due diligence) of the company you're buying. For example, you (or a competent financial/tax person) need to analyze the existing business's financial statements to ascertain whether

the company really is as profitable as it appears and to determine its current financial health.

>> **You lack capital:** Why do a lot of people start a business instead of buying one? Because they simply don't have enough cash — or credit potential — to buy one. Although you may feel like you're more the business-buying type than the business-starting type, if you don't have the necessary dough, and if you can't find investors or lenders to provide it, then your avenue to business ownership may be decided for you, regardless of the avenue you'd prefer.

>> **You think you'll miss out on the satisfaction of creating a business:** Whether it nourishes their souls or simply gratifies their egos, entrepreneurs who build their own businesses get a different rush than those who buy existing companies. Certainly you can make your mark on a business you buy, but doing so takes a number of years. Even then, the business is never completely your own creation.

Chapter **6**

Raking in Profits from Real Estate

Real estate is one of the three time-tested ways for people of varied economic means to build wealth (the others are stocks and small business, covered in Chapters 3–5). Over the long term (decades), you should be able to make an average annualized return of 8 to 9 percent per year investing in real estate.

Investing in real estate isn't rocket science but does require doing your homework. If you're sloppy doing your legwork, you're more likely to end up with inferior properties or to overpay. This chapter concentrates more on residential investment opportunities, which are more accessible and appropriate for nonexperts.

Although you should make money over the long term investing in good real estate properties, you *can* lose money, especially in the short term. Don't unrealistically expect real estate values to increase every year. Downturns in the local real estate prices may create temporary buying opportunities, but we aren't real estate day traders. When you invest in real estate for the long term, the occasional price declines should be merely bumps on an otherwise fruitful journey.

Homeownership: Building Equity One Brick at a Time

Even though your home consumes a lot of dough (mortgage payments, property taxes, insurance, maintenance, and so on) while you own it, it can help you accomplish important financial goals:

>> **Retiring:** By the time you hit your 50s and 60s, the size of your monthly mortgage payment, relative to your income and assets, should start to look small or nonexistent. Lowered housing costs can help you afford to retire or cut back from full-time work. Some people choose to sell their homes and buy less-costly ones or to rent out the homes and live on some or all of the cash in retirement. Other homeowners enhance their retirement income by taking out a reverse mortgage to tap the equity that they've built up in their properties.

>> **Pursuing your small-business dreams:** Running your own business can be a source of great satisfaction. Financial barriers, however, prevent many people from pulling the plug on a regular job and taking the entrepreneurial plunge. You may be able to borrow against the equity that you've built up in your home to get the cash you need to start your own business. Depending on what type of business you have in mind, you may even be able to run your enterprise from your home.

>> **Financing college/higher education:** It may seem like only yesterday that your kids were born, but soon enough, they'll be ready for an expensive four-year undertaking: college. Of course, there are alternatives. Borrowing against the equity in your home is a viable way to help pay for your kids' higher-education costs.

Perhaps you won't use your home's equity for retirement, a small business, educational expenses, or other important financial goals. But even if you decide to pass your home on to your children, a charity, or a long-lost relative, it's still a valuable asset and a worthwhile investment.

Of course, before you can start building up equity in a home, you have to buy one. This section discusses some of the main things to consider when purchasing a home.

Weighing the pros and cons of ownership

Some people — particularly enthusiastic salespeople in the real estate business — believe everybody should own a home. You may hear them say things like "Buy a home for the tax breaks" or "Renting is like throwing your money away."

REMEMBER

The bulk of home ownership costs — namely, mortgage interest and property taxes — are tax-deductible subject to limitations. However, these tax breaks are already largely factored into the higher cost of owning a home. So, don't buy a home just because of the tax breaks.

Renting isn't necessarily equal to "throwing your money away." In fact, renting can have a number of benefits, such as the following:

» **In some communities, with a given type of property, renting is less costly than buying.** Happy and successful renters I've seen include people who pay low rent, perhaps because they've made housing sacrifices. If you can sock away 10 percent or more of your earnings while renting, you're probably well on your way to accomplishing your future financial goals.

» **You can save money and hopefully invest in other financial assets.** Stocks, bonds, and mutual and exchange-traded funds are quite accessible and useful in retirement. Some long-term homeowners, by contrast, have a substantial portion of their wealth tied up in their homes. However, accessibility is a double-edged sword because it may tempt you, as a cash-rich renter, to blow the money in the short term.

» **Renting has potential emotional and psychological rewards.** The main reward is the not-so-inconsequential fact that you have more flexibility to pack up and move on. You may have a lease to fulfill, but you may be able to renegotiate it if you need to move on. As a homeowner, you have a major monthly payment to take care of. To some people, this responsibility feels like a financial ball and chain. After all, you have no guarantee that you can sell your home in a timely fashion or at the price you desire if you want to move.

Although renting has its benefits, renting has at least one big drawback: exposure to inflation. As the cost of living increases, your landlord can keep increasing your rent (unless you live in a rent-controlled unit). If you're a homeowner, however, the big monthly expense of the mortgage payment doesn't increase, assuming that you buy your home with a fixed-rate mortgage. (Your property taxes, homeowners insurance, and maintenance expenses are exposed to inflation, but these expenses are usually much smaller in comparison to your monthly mortgage payment or rent.)

Knowing when to buy

If you're considering buying a home, you may be concerned about whether home prices are poised to rise or fall. No one wants to purchase a home that then plummets in value. And who wouldn't like to buy just before prices go on an upward trajectory?

It's not easy to predict what's going to happen with real estate prices in a particular city or region over the next one, two, three, or more years. Ultimately, an area's economic health and vitality drive the demand and prices for homes in that area. An increase in jobs, particularly ones that pay well, increases the demand for housing. And when demand goes up, so do prices.

If you first buy a home when you're in your 20s, 30s, or even your 40s, you may end up as a homeowner for several decades. Over such a long time, you may experience numerous ups and downs. But you'll probably see more ups than downs, so don't be overly concerned about trying to predict what's going to happen to the real estate market in the near term. I know some long-term renters who avoided buying homes decades ago because they thought that prices were high. Consequently, they missed out on tremendous appreciation in real estate values. (The one silver lining to the late 2000s decline in home prices is that homes became more affordable than they had been in a long time.)

That said, at particular times in your life, you may be ambivalent about buying a home. Perhaps you're not sure whether you'll stay put for more than three to five years. Therefore, part of your home-buying decision may hinge on whether current home prices in your local area offer you a good value. The state of the job market, the number of home listings for sale, and the level of real estate prices as compared to rent are useful indicators of the housing market's health. Trying to time your purchase has more importance if you think you may move in less than five years. In that case, avoid buying in a market where home prices are relatively high compared to their rental costs. If you expect to move so soon, renting generally makes more sense because of the high transaction costs of buying and selling real estate.

Recouping transaction costs

Financially speaking, I recommend that you wait to buy a home until you can see yourself staying put for a minimum of three years. Ideally, I'd like you to think that you have a good shot of staying in the home for five or more years. Why? Buying and selling a home cost big bucks, and you generally need at least five years of low appreciation to recoup your transaction costs. Some of the expenses you face when buying and selling a home include the following:

>> **Inspection fees:** You shouldn't buy a property without thoroughly checking it out, so you'll incur inspection expenses. Good inspectors can help you identify problems with the plumbing, heating, and electrical systems. They also check out the foundation, roof, and so on. They can even tell you whether termites are living in the house. Property inspections typically range from a few hundred dollars up to $1,000+ for larger homes.

>> **Loan costs:** The costs of getting a mortgage include items such as the *points* (up-front interest that can run 1 to 2 percent of the loan amount), application and credit report fees, and appraisal fees.

>> **Title insurance:** When you buy a home, you and your lender need to protect yourselves against the chance — albeit small — that the property seller doesn't actually legally own the home you're buying. That's where title insurance comes in — it protects you financially from unscrupulous sellers. Title insurance costs vary by area; 0.5 percent of the purchase price of the property is about average.

>> **Moving costs:** You can transport all your furniture, clothing, and other personal belongings yourself, but your time is worth something, and your moving skills may be limited. Besides, do you want to end up in a hospital emergency room after being pinned at the bottom of a staircase by a

runaway couch? Moving costs vary wildly, but you can count on spending hundreds to thousands of dollars. (You can get a ballpark idea of moving costs from a number of online calculators.)

>> **Real estate agents' commissions:** A commission of 5 to 7 percent of the purchase price of most homes is paid to the real estate salespeople and the companies they work for. Higher priced homes generally qualify for lower commission rates.

REMEMBER

On top of all these transaction costs of buying and then selling a home, you'll also face maintenance expenses — for example, fixing leaky pipes and painting. To cover typical transaction and maintenance costs of home ownership, the value of your home needs to appreciate about 15 percent over the years that you own it for you to be as well off financially as if you had continued renting. Fifteen percent! If you need or want to move elsewhere in a few years, counting on that kind of appreciation in those few years is risky. If you happen to buy just before a sharp rise in housing prices, you may get this much appreciation in a short time. But you can't count on this upswing — you're more likely to lose money on such a short-term deal.

Some people invest in real estate even when they don't expect to live in the home for long, and they may consider turning their home into a rental if they move within a few years. Doing so can work well financially in the long haul, but don't underestimate the responsibilities that come with rental property.

REMEMBER

When you finally buy a home, be sure to refigure how much you need to pay in income tax because your mortgage interest and property tax deductions can help lower your tax bill. Many new homebuyers don't bother with this step, and they receive a big tax refund on their next filed income tax return. Although getting money back from the IRS may feel good, it means that at a minimum, you gave the IRS an interest-free loan. In the worst-case scenario, the reduced cash flow during the year may cause you to accumulate debt or miss out on contributing to tax-deductible retirement accounts.

For a precise estimate as to how home ownership may affect your tax situation, get out your tax return and plug in some reasonable numbers to guesstimate how your taxes may change. You can also speak with a tax advisor.

Deciding how much to spend

Buying a home is a long-term financial commitment. You'll probably take out a 15- or 30-year mortgage to finance your purchase, and the home you buy will need maintenance over the years. So, before you decide to buy, take stock of your overall financial health.

If you have good credit and a reliable source of employment, lenders will eagerly offer to loan you money. They'll tell you how much you may borrow from them — the maximum that you're qualified to borrow. Just because they offer you that maximum amount, however, doesn't mean you should borrow the maximum. Lenders don't consider the other monthly expenses of home ownership; you must account for these expenses (and your other financial goals) on your own.

Buying a home without considering your other monthly expenditures and long-term goals may cause you to end up with a home that dictates much of your future spending. Have you considered, for example, how much you need to save monthly to reach your retirement goals? How about the amount you want to spend on recreation and entertainment?

If you want to continue your current lifestyle, you have to be honest with yourself about how much you can really afford to spend as a homeowner. First-time home buyers in particular run into financial trouble when they don't understand their current spending. Buying a home can be a wise decision, but it can also be a huge burden. And you can buy all sorts of nifty things for a home. Some people prop up their spending habits with credit cards — a dangerous practice.

Don't let your home control your financial future. Before you buy a property or agree to a particular mortgage, be sure you can afford to do so — be especially careful not to ignore your retirement planning (if you hope to someday retire).

Determining your down payment

When deciding how much to borrow for a home, keep in mind that most lenders require you to purchase *private mortgage insurance* (PMI) if your down payment is less than 20 percent of your home's purchase price. PMI protects the lender from getting stuck with a property that may be worth less than the mortgage you owe, in the event that you default on your loan. On a moderate-size loan, PMI can add hundreds of dollars per year to your payments.

If you have to take PMI to buy a home with less than 20 percent down, keep an eye on your home's value and your loan balance. Over time, your property should appreciate, and your loan balance should decrease as you make monthly payments. After your mortgage represents 80 percent or less of the market value of the home, you can get rid of the PMI. Doing so usually entails contacting your lender and paying for an appraisal.

I have never been a fan of *interest-only* loans, which entice cash-strapped buyers with lower monthly payments, because all the initial payments go toward interest. These loans typically have worse *terms* (interest rate and fees) than conventional mortgages and cause some buyers to take on more debt than they can handle. After a number of years, the payment amount jumps higher when the principal and interest begin to be repaid together.

What if you have so much money that you can afford to make more than a 20 percent down payment? How much should you put down then? (This problem doesn't usually arise — most buyers, especially first-time buyers, struggle to get a 20 percent down payment together.) The answer depends on what else you can or want to do with the money. If you're considering other investment opportunities, determine whether you can expect to earn a higher rate of return on those other investments versus the interest rate that you'd pay on the mortgage. Forget about the tax deduction for your mortgage interest. Subject to limitations, mortgage interest is deductible, but remember that the earnings from your investments are ultimately taxable.

During the past century, stock market and real estate investors have enjoyed average annual returns of around 9 percent per year. So, if you borrow mortgage money at around 5 to 6 percent, in the long term, you may come out a few percent ahead if you use the money you would have put toward a larger down payment to invest in such growth investments. You aren't guaranteed, of course, that your investments will earn 9 percent yearly. (Remember that past returns don't guarantee the future.) And don't forget that all investments come with risk. The advantage of putting more money down and borrowing less is that it's essentially a risk-free investment (as long as you have adequate insurance on your property).

TIP

If you prefer to put down just 20 percent and invest more money elsewhere, that's fine. Just don't keep the extra money (beyond an emergency reserve) under the mattress, in a savings account, or in bonds that pay less interest than your mortgage costs you in interest. Invest in stocks, real estate, or a small business. Otherwise, you don't have a chance at earning a higher return than the cost of your mortgage and therefore, will be better off paying down your mortgage.

Selecting your property type

If you're ready to buy a home, you must make some decisions about what and where to buy. If you grew up in the suburbs, your image of a home may include the traditional single-family home with a lawn, kids, and family pets. But single-family homes, of course, aren't the only or even the main type of residential housing in many areas, especially in some higher-cost, urban neighborhoods. Other common types of higher-density ("shared") housing include the following:

>> **Condominiums:** *Condominiums* are generally apartment-style units that are stacked on top of and adjacent to one another. Many condo buildings were originally apartments that were converted — through the sale of ownership of separate units — into condos. When you purchase a condominium, you purchase a specific unit as well as a share of the common areas (for example, the pool, landscaping, entry and hallways, laundry room, and so on).

>> **Townhomes:** *Townhome* is just a fancy way of saying attached or row home. Think of a townhome as a cross between a condominium and a single-family house. Townhomes are condo-like because they're attached (generally sharing walls and a roof) and are homelike because they're often two-story buildings that come with a small yard.

>> **Cooperatives:** *Cooperatives* (usually called co-ops) resemble apartment and condominium buildings. When you buy a share in a cooperative, you own a share of the entire building, including some living space. Unlike in a condo, you generally need to get approval from the cooperative association if you want to remodel or rent your unit to a

tenant. In some co-ops, you must even gain approval from the association for the sale of your unit to a proposed buyer. Co-ops are generally much harder to obtain loans for and to sell, so I don't recommend that you buy one unless you get a good deal and can easily obtain a loan.

REMEMBER

All types of shared housing in the preceding list offer two potential advantages:

>> **This type of housing generally gives you more living space for your dollars.** This value makes sense because with a single-family home, a good chunk of the property's cost is for the land that the home sits on. Land is good for decks, recreation, and playing children, but you don't live "in" it the way you do with your home. Shared housing maximizes living space for the housing dollars you spend.

>> **In many situations, you're not personally responsible for general maintenance.** Instead, the homeowners association (which you pay into) takes care of it. If you don't have the time, energy, or desire to keep up a property, shared housing can make sense. Shared housing units may also give you access to recreation facilities, such as a pool, tennis/pickleball courts, and exercise equipment.

So why doesn't everyone purchase shared housing? Well, as investments, single-family homes generally outperform other housing types. Shared housing is easier to build (and to over-build) — and the greater supply tends to keep its prices from rising as much. Single-family homes tend to attract more potential buyers — most people, when they can afford it, prefer a stand-alone home, especially for the increased privacy.

TIP

If you can afford a smaller single-family home instead of a larger shared-housing unit and don't shudder at the thought of maintaining a home, buy the single-family home. Shared housing makes more sense for people who don't want to deal with building maintenance and who value the security of living in a larger building with other people. Keep in mind that shared-housing prices tend to hold up better in developed urban environments. If possible, avoid shared housing units in suburban areas where the availability of developable land makes building many more units possible, thus increasing the supply of housing and slowing growth in values.

If shared housing interests you, make sure you have the property thoroughly inspected. Also, examine the trend in maintenance fees over time to ensure that these costs are under control.

Building Wealth through Real Estate Investing

Compared with most other investments, good real estate can excel at producing periodic or monthly cash flow for property owners. So, in addition to the longer-term appreciation potential, you can also earn investment income year in and year out. Real estate is a true growth *and* income investment.

The following list highlights the major benefits of investing in real estate:

>> **Tax-deferred compounding of value:** In real estate investing, the appreciation of your properties compounds *tax-deferred* during your years of ownership. You don't pay tax on this appreciation/profit until you sell your property — and even then, with some careful planning, you may be able to roll over your gain into another investment property and avoid paying taxes. (See the "Being aware of the tax advantages" section later in this chapter.)

>> **Regular cash flow:** If you have property that you rent out, you have money coming in every month in the form of rents. Some properties, particularly larger multi-unit complexes, may have some additional sources, such as from parking, storage, or laundry equipment.

REMEMBER

When you own investment real estate, you should also expect to incur expenses that include your mortgage payment, property taxes, insurance, and maintenance. The interaction of the revenues coming in and the expenses going out is what tells you whether you realize a positive operating cash flow each month.

>> **Reduced income tax bills:** For income tax purposes, you also get to claim an expense that isn't really an out-of-pocket cost — depreciation. Depreciation enables you to reduce your current income tax bill and hence increase your cash flow from a property. (Check out the "Being aware of the tax advantages" section for more info.)

>> **Rate of increase of rental income versus overall expenses:** While not always true in recent years, often over time, your operating cash flow and even your net profit, which is subject to ordinary income tax, should rise as you increase your rental prices faster than the rate of increase for your property's overall expenses. What follows is a simple example to show why even modest rental increases are magnified into larger operating profits and healthy returns on investment over time.

Suppose that you're in the market to purchase a single-family home that you want to rent out and that such properties are selling for about $300,000 in the area you've deemed to be a good investment. (*Note:* Housing prices vary widely across different areas, but the following example should give you a relative sense of how a rental property's expenses and revenue change over time.) You expect to make a 20 percent down payment and take out a 30-year fixed rate mortgage at 6 percent for the remainder of the purchase price — $240,000. Here are the details:

Monthly mortgage payment	$1,440
Monthly property tax	$300
Other monthly expenses (maintenance, insurance)	$300
Monthly rent	$2,100

In Table 6-1, you can see what happens with your investment over time. It's assumed that your rent and expenses (except for your mortgage payment, which is fixed) increase 3 percent annually and that your property appreciates a conservative 4 percent per year. (For simplification purposes, depreciation is ignored in this example. If the benefit of depreciation had been included, it would further enhance the calculated investment returns.)

TABLE 6-1 How a Rental Property's Income and Wealth Build Over Time

Year	Monthly Rent	Monthly Expenses	Property Value	Mortgage Balance
0	$2,100	$2,040	$300,000	$240,000
5	$2,434	$2,136	$364,995	$223,440
10	$2,821	$2,247	$444,075	$200,880
20	$3,793	$2,523	$657,337	$129,600
30	$5,097	$2,896	$973,020	$0
31	$5,250	$1,500	$1,011,937	$0

Now, notice what happens over time. When you first buy the property, the monthly rent and the monthly expenses are about equal. By year five, the monthly income exceeds the expenses by about $300 per month. Consider why this happens — your largest monthly expense, the mortgage payment, doesn't increase. So, even though the rent is assumed to increase just 3 percent per year, which is the same rate of increase assumed for your non-mortgage expenses, the compounding of rental inflation begins to produce larger and larger cash flows to you, the property owner. Cash flow of $300 per month may not sound like much, but consider that this $3,600 annual income is from an original $60,000 investment. Thus, by year five, your rental property is producing a 6 percent return on your down payment investment. (And remember, if you factor in the tax deduction for depreciation, your cash flow and return are even higher.)

In addition to the monthly cash flow from the amount that the rent exceeds the property's expenses, also look at the last two columns in Table 1-1 to see what has happened by year five to your *equity* (the difference between market value and mortgage balance owed) in the property. With just a 4 percent annual increase in market value, your $60,000 in equity (the down payment) has more than doubled to $141,555 ($364,995 − $223,440).

By years 10 and 20, you can see the further increases in your monthly cash flow and significant expansion in your property's equity. By year 30, the property is producing more than $2,200 per month cash flow and you're now the proud owner of a mortgage-free property worth more than triple what you paid for it!

After you get the mortgage paid off in year 30, take a look at what happens in year 31 and beyond to your monthly expenses (big drop as your monthly mortgage payment disappears!) and therefore, your cash flow (big increase).

Recognizing the drawbacks of real estate investing

Purchasing and owning investment real estate and being a landlord are time consuming. The same way an uninformed owner can sell his property for less than it's worth, if you fail to do your homework before purchasing property, you can end up overpaying or buying real estate with problems. Finding competent and ethical real estate professionals takes time. Investigating communities, neighborhoods, and zoning also soaks up plenty of hours, as does examining tenant issues with potential properties.

As for managing a property, you can hire a property manager to interview tenants, collect the rent, and solve problems such as leaky faucets and broken appliances, but doing so costs money and still requires some of your time. Of course, if you hire a competent and experienced property manager, you will be rewarded with less time required for oversight.

REMEMBER

If you're stretched too thin due to work and family responsibilities, real estate investing may not be for you. So, unless you want to locate, interview, hire, and pay for a qualified property manager, you may want to look into a less time-intensive real estate investments, such as REITs, which I cover later in this chapter.

Despite all its potential, real estate investing isn't lucrative at all times and for all people — here's a quick outline of the biggest caveats that accompany investing in real estate:

>> **Few home runs:** Your likely returns from real estate won't approach the biggest home runs that the most accomplished entrepreneurs achieve in the business world. That

said, by doing your homework, improving properties, and practicing good management (and sometimes enjoying a bit of luck), you can do extremely well!

WARNING

» **Up-front operating profit challenges:** Unless you make a large down payment, your monthly operating profit may be small, nonexistent, or negative in the early years of rental property ownership. During soft periods in the local economy, rents may rise more slowly than your expenses or they may even fall. That's why you must ensure that you can weather financially tough times. In the worst cases, we've seen rental property owners lose both their investment property and their homes.

» **Ups and downs:** You're not going to earn an 8 to 9 percent return every year. Although you have the potential for significant profits, owning real estate isn't like owning a printing press at the U.S. Treasury. Like stocks and other types of ownership investments, real estate goes through down periods as well as up periods. Most people who make money investing in real estate do so because they invest and hold property over many years.

» **Relatively high transaction costs:** If you buy a property and then want out a year or two later, you may find that even though the property has appreciated in value, much (if not all) of your profit has been wiped away by the high transaction costs. Typically, the costs of buying and selling — which include real estate agent commissions, loan fees, title insurance, and other closing costs — amount to about 8 to 12 percent of the purchase price of a property. So, although you may be elated if your property appreciates 10 percent in value in short order, you may not be so thrilled to realize that if you sell the property, you may not have any greater return than if you had stashed your money in a lowly, risk-free, FDIC-insured bank account.

» **Tax implications:** Last, but not least, when you make a positive net return or profit on your real estate investment, the federal and state governments are waiting with open hands for their share. Throughout this book, I highlight ways to improve your after-tax returns. As stressed more than once, the profit you have left after government entities take their bites (not your pretax income) is what really matters.

These drawbacks shouldn't keep you from exploring real estate investing as an option; rather, they simply reinforce the need to really know what you're getting into with this type of investing and whether it's a good match for you.

Comparing real estate to other investments

Surely, you've considered or heard about many different investments over the years. To help you grasp and understand the unique characteristics of real estate, this section compares and contrasts real estate's attributes with those of other wealth-building investments like stocks and small business.

Returns

Clearly, a major reason that many people invest in real estate is for the healthy total *returns* (which include ongoing cash flow and the appreciation of the property). Real estate often generates robust long-term returns because, like stocks and small business, it's an *ownership investment.* By that, I mean that real estate is an asset that has the ability to produce periodic income *and* gains or profits upon refinancing or sale.

Our research and experience suggest that total real estate investment returns are comparable to those from stocks — about 8 to 9 percent on average, annually. Over recent decades, the average annual return on real estate investment trusts (REITs), publicly traded companies that invest in income-producing real estate such as apartment buildings, office complexes, and shopping centers, has appreciated at about this pace as well. See the discussion of REITs later in this chapter.

And you can earn long-term returns that average 10+ percent per year if you select excellent properties in the best areas, hold them for several years, and manage them well.

Risk

Real estate doesn't always rise in value — witness the decline in most parts of the United States during the great real estate recession of 2008–2012. That said, while interest-rate sensitive, real-estate market values generally don't suffer from as much volatility as stock prices do.

Keep in mind (especially if you tend to be concerned about shorter-term risks) that real estate can suffer from declines of 10 percent, 20 percent, or more. If you make a down payment of, say, 20 percent and want to sell your property after a 10 to 15 percent price decline, you may find that all (as in 100 percent) of your invested dollars (down payment) are wiped out after you factor in transaction costs. So, you can lose everything.

REMEMBER

You can greatly reduce and minimize your risk investing in real estate through buying and holding property for many years (seven to ten or more). Remember that many of these fantastic success stories about amazing profits on "flipping" single-family homes and small rental properties are just like gamblers who only tell you about their biggest winnings or forget to tell you that they turned around and lost much of what they won. While there is a lot of hype on television, streaming content, and the internet about "flipping properties" for crazy short-term profits, think of real estate as a long-term investment.

Liquidity

Liquidity — the ease and cost with which you can sell and get your money out of an investment — is one of real estate's short-comings. Real estate is relatively *illiquid:* You can't sell a piece of property with the same speed with which you can whip out your ATM card and withdraw money from your bank account or sell a stock or an exchange-traded fund with a click of your computer's mouse or by tapping on your smart phone.

REMEMBER

I actually view real estate's relative illiquidity as a strength, certainly compared with stocks that people often trade in and out of because doing so is so easy and seemingly cheap. As a result, some stock market investors tend to lose sight of the long term and miss out on the bigger gains that accrue to patient buy-and-stick-with-it investors. Because you can't track the value of investment real estate daily online, and because real estate takes considerable time, energy, and money to sell, you're far more likely to buy and hold onto your properties for the longer term.

Although real estate investments are generally less liquid than stocks, they're generally more liquid than investments made in your own or someone else's small business. People need a place to live and businesses need a place to operate, so there's always demand for real estate (although the supply of such available properties can greatly exceed the demand in some areas during certain time periods).

Capital requirements

Although you can easily get started with traditional investments such as stocks and mutual funds with a few hundred or thousand dollars, the vast majority of quality real estate investments require far greater investments — usually on the order of tens of thousands of dollars.

TIP

If you're one of the many people who don't have that kind of money, don't despair. I present you with lower-cost real estate investment options. Among the simplest low-cost real estate investment options are real estate investment trusts (REITs). You can buy these as exchange-traded stocks or invest in a portfolio of REITs through a REIT mutual fund (see the upcoming section about REITs).

Diversification value

An advantage of holding investment real estate is that its value doesn't necessarily move in tandem with other investments, such as stocks or small-business investments that you hold. You may recall, for example, the massive stock market decline in the early 2000s. In most communities around America, real estate values were either steady or actually rising during this horrendous period for stock prices.

However, real estate prices and stock prices, for example, *can* move down together in value (witness the severe recession and stock market drop that took hold in 2008). Sluggish business conditions and lower corporate profits can depress stock *and* real estate prices.

Opportunities to add value

Although you may not know much about investing in the stock market, you may have some good ideas about how to improve a property and make it more valuable. You can fix up a property or develop it further and raise the rental income accordingly. Perhaps through legwork, persistence, and good negotiating skills, you can purchase a property below its fair market value.

Relative to investing in the stock market, tenacious and savvy real estate investors can more easily buy property in the private real estate market at below fair market value because the real estate market is somewhat less efficient, and some owners don't realize the value of their income property or they need to sell quickly. Theoretically, you can do the same in the stock market, but the scores of professional, full-time money managers who analyze the public market for stocks make finding bargains more difficult and even elusive.

Being aware of the tax advantages

Real estate investment offers numerous tax advantages. This section compares and contrasts investment property tax issues with those of other investments.

>> **Deductible expenses (including depreciation):** Owning a property has much in common with owning your own small business. Every year, you account for your income and expenses on a tax return. One expense that you get to deduct for rental real estate on your tax return — depreciation — doesn't actually involve spending or outlaying money. *Depreciation* is an allowable tax deduction for buildings because structures wear out over time. Under current tax laws, residential real estate is depreciated over 27½ years (commercial buildings are less favored in the tax code and can be depreciated over 39 years). Residential real estate is depreciated over shorter time periods because it has traditionally been a favored investment in our nation's tax laws.

>> **Tax-free rollovers of rental property profits:** When you sell a stock, mutual fund, or exchange-traded investment that you hold outside a retirement account, you must pay tax on your net gains or profits. By contrast, you can avoid paying tax on your profit when you sell a rental property if you roll over your gain into another like-kind investment real estate property.

The rules for properly making one of these exchanges (called *1031 exchanges*) are complex and involve third parties. Make sure that you find an attorney and/or tax advisor who is an expert at these transactions to ensure that you meet the technical and strict timing requirements so everything goes smoothly (and legally).

If you don't roll over your net gain, you may owe significant taxes because of how the IRS defines your gain.

>> **Deferred taxes with installment sales:** *Installment sales* are a complex method that can be used to defer your tax bill when you sell an investment property at a profit and you don't buy another rental property. With such a sale, you play the role of banker and provide financing to the buyer. In addition to often collecting a competitive interest rate from the buyer, you only have to pay capital gains tax as you receive proceeds over time from the sale that are applied toward the principal or price the buyer agreed to pay for the property.

>> **Special tax credits for low-income housing and old buildings:** If you invest in and upgrade low-income housing or certified historic buildings, you can gain special tax credits. The credits represent a direct reduction in your tax bill from expenditures to rehabilitate and improve such properties. These tax credits exist to encourage investors to invest in and fix up old or run-down buildings that likely would continue to deteriorate otherwise. The IRS has strict rules governing what types of properties qualify. See IRS Form 3468 to discover more about these credits.

The 2017 Tax Cuts and Jobs Act created "qualified opportunity zones" to provide tax incentives to invest in "low-income communities," which are defined by each state's governor and may comprise up to 25 percent of designated "low-income communities" in each state. (States can also designate census tracts contiguous with "low-income communities" so long as the median family income in those tracts doesn't exceed 125 percent of the qualifying contiguous "low-income community.")

>> **Twenty percent Qualified Business Income (QBI) deduction for "pass-through entities":** The Tax Cuts and Jobs Act included lower across-the-board federal income tax rates, which benefits all wage earners and investors, including real estate investors. If you spend at least 250 hours per year on certain activities related to your real estate investments, you may also be able to utilize an additional tax break targeted to certain small-business entities.

Considering REITs (Real Estate Investment Trusts)

Real estate investment trusts (REITs) are for-profit companies that own and generally operate different types of property. The options for REIT investments are extremely broad and cover virtually every type of real estate. You can choose your favorite REIT from the following income property types:

>> **Office:** Ranging from Class "A" prestigious urban skyscrapers with high quality finishes and amenities, to Class "B" well-located with standard finishes, to single-story or low-rise suburban, functional Class "C" buildings with few or no amenities

>> **Residential:** Apartments, student housing, manufactured homes, multi-family 2–4 units, single-family homes

>> **Retail:** Regional malls, big box, outlet centers, grocery-anchored shopping centers, strip centers

>> **Industrial:** Warehouses, distribution centers, production, assembly, manufacturing, research

>> **Hospitality:** Hotels, resorts, lodging, restaurant, bars and pubs, spa and wellness centers, travel centers, conference centers, music venues, wedding venues

>> **Healthcare:** Hospitals, medical/dental office buildings, senior living facilities, skilled nursing and memory care facilities

>> **Self-storage:** Drive-up units, climate-controlled units, 24-hour facilities

>> **Cell towers:** Rural and national providers

>> **Other rental income properties, even timberlands**

These property-holding REITs are known as *equity REITs.* Some REITs, known as *mortgage REITs* (or *mREITs*), focus on the financing end of the business; they lend to real estate property owners and operators or provide credit indirectly through buying loans (mortgage-backed securities).

TIP

Equity REIT managers typically identify and negotiate the purchase of properties that they believe are good investments and manage these properties directly or through an affiliated advisory and management company, including all tenant relations. Thus, REITs can be a good way to invest in real estate for people who don't want the hassles and headaches that come with directly owning and managing rental property. You can also invest in different property type REITs to diversify your portfolio, but check their returns and expense ratios as not all REITs within the same property type field are equivalent. This is similar to the reality that while most mutual funds all invest in the same pool of NYSE listed stocks, not all have the same expenses or results.

Distinguishing between public and private REITs

Don't be shy about asking for full disclosure of the relationship between the REIT, its advisors, and the management companies. REITs often involve conflicts of interest that aren't clearly disclosed or pay significant above-market fees to directly or indirectly related entities or affiliates that ultimately lower the cash flow and return on investment available for distribution.

Public REITs are traded on the major stock exchanges, and thus must meet strict SEC reporting requirements:

>> **Liquidity:** Public REITs trade every business day on a stock exchange, and thus offer investors the ability to buy and sell as they please. Of course, as with other similarly liquid investments (like stock in companies in a variety of industries), liquidity can have its downside. More-liquid real estate investments like REITs may inspire frequent trades caused by making emotional decisions or trying to time market movements.

>> **Independent board of directors:** A public company must have directors, the majority of whom are independent of its management. Shareholders vote upon and elect these directors, but that is no guarantee of their competency.

>> **Financial reporting:** Public REITs, like other public companies, must file comprehensive financial reports quarterly.

I recommend that you stay away from private REITs unless you're a sophisticated, experienced real estate investor willing to do plenty of extra research and digging. Because they're not publicly traded, private REITs don't have the same disclosure requirements as public REITs. This difference means an investor in a private REIT had better carefully scrutinize the prospectus and realize that the private REIT has the ability to make changes that may not be in the investor's best interests but that reward the private REIT sponsors or their affiliates.

Taking a look at performance

So what about performance? Over the long term, REITs have produced total returns comparable to stocks in general. In fact, REIT returns historically have been comparable to stock returns. In the context of an overall investment portfolio, REITs add diversification because their values don't always move in tandem with other investments. Having a diversified and balanced portfolio of different asset classes that react independently of one another can mitigate some of the risk and allow you to achieve overall higher returns on your investments.

One final attribute of REITs I want to highlight is the fairly substantial dividends that REITs usually pay. Because these dividends are generally fully taxable (and thus not eligible for the lower stock dividend tax rate), you should generally avoid holding REITs outside of retirement accounts if you're in a high tax bracket (for instance, during your prime working years).

Investing in REIT funds

You can research and purchase shares in individual REITs, which trade as securities on the major stock exchanges. An even better approach is to buy a mutual fund or exchange-traded fund that invests in a diversified mixture of REITs. Some of the best REIT mutual funds charge 1 percent per year or less in management fees and have long-term track records of success while taking modest risks. Vanguard's Real Estate Index Fund charges just 0.13 percent per year in fees and has produced average annual returns of about 8.8 percent since its inception in 2001.

Vanguard also offers a REIT ETF (exchange-traded fund) through most discount brokers and boasts a low management fee of 0.13 percent. (You can buy it without any brokerage fees through Vanguard and other leading brokers that offer commission-free stock and ETF trades.)

In addition to providing you with a diversified, low-hassle real estate investment, REITs offer an additional advantage that traditional rental real estate doesn't. You can easily invest in REITs through a retirement account such as an IRA. As with traditional real estate investments, you can even buy REITs and mutual fund REITs with borrowed money (in nonretirement accounts). Although risky, you can buy with 50 percent down, known as *buying on margin,* when you purchase such investments through a brokerage account.

Chapter **7**

Cutting Your Taxes (Keeping More of What You Earn)

The tax system is built around incentives to encourage desirable behavior and activity. Homeownership, for example, is considered good because it encourages people to take more responsibility for maintaining properties and neighborhoods. Therefore, the government offers numerous tax benefits, referred to as *allowable deductions,* to encourage people to own homes. But if you don't understand these tax benefits, you probably don't know how to take full advantage of them, either.

Don't feel dumb when it comes to understanding the tax system. You're not the problem — the complexity of the income tax system is. Making sense of the tax jungle is more daunting than hacking your way out of a triple-canopy rainforest with a dinner knife. That's why, throughout this book, I help you understand the tax system, and I promise not to make you read the actual tax laws.

You should be able to keep more of your money by applying the tax-reducing strategies I present in this chapter.

Reducing Taxes on Work Income

When you earn money from work, you're supposed to pay income tax on that income. Some people avoid taxes by illegal means, such as by not reporting work income (which isn't really possible if you're getting a regular paycheck from an employer), but you can very well end up paying a heap of penalties and extra interest charges on top of the taxes you owe. And you may even get tossed in jail. This section focuses on the legal ways to reduce your income taxes on work-related income.

Self-employed workers and business owners also must pay income tax, but their situations are subject to some unique rules and can be a bit more complex.

Contributing to retirement investment plans

A retirement investment plan is one of the few relatively painless and authorized ways to reduce your taxable employment income. Besides reducing your taxes, retirement plans help you build up a nest egg so you don't have to work for the rest of your life.

You can exclude money from your taxable income by tucking it away in employer-based retirement plans, such as 401(k) or 403(b) accounts, or self-employed retirement plans, such as SEP-IRAs. If your combined federal and state marginal tax rate is, say, 33 percent and you contribute $1,000 to one of these plans, you reduce your federal and state taxes by $330. Do you like the sound of that? How about this: Contribute another $1,000, and your taxes drop *another* $330 (as long as you're still in the same marginal tax rate). And when your money is inside a retirement account, it can compound and grow without taxation.

WARNING

Many people miss this great opportunity to reduce their taxes because they *spend* all (or too much) of their current employment income and, therefore, have nothing (or little) left to put into a retirement account. If you're in this predicament, you first need to reduce your spending before you can contribute money to a retirement plan.

If your employer doesn't offer the option of saving money through a retirement plan, lobby the benefits and human resources departments. If they resist, you may want to add this to your list of reasons for considering another employer. Many employers offer this valuable benefit, but some don't. Some company decision-makers either don't understand the value of these accounts or feel that they're too costly to set up and administer.

If your employer doesn't offer a retirement savings plan, individual retirement account (IRA) contributions may or may not be tax-deductible, depending on your circumstances. You should first maximize contributions to the previously mentioned tax-deductible accounts.

TIP

Lower- and moderate-income earners can gain a federal tax credit known as the "Saver's Credit." Married couples filing jointly with adjusted gross incomes (AGIs) of less than $76,500 and single taxpayers with an AGI of less than $38,250 can earn a tax credit (claimed on Form 8880) for retirement account contributions. Unlike a deduction, a *tax credit* directly reduces your tax bill by the amount of the credit. This credit, which is detailed in Table 7-1, is a percentage of the first $2,000 contributed (or $4,000 on a joint return). The credit is not available to those under the age of 18, full-time students, or people who are claimed as dependents on someone else's tax return.

TABLE 7-1 Special Tax Credit for Retirement Plan Contributions

Singles Adjusted Gross Income	Married-Filing-Jointly Adjusted Gross Income	Tax Credit for Retirement Account Contributions
$0–$23,750	$0–$47,500	50%
$23,750–$25,500	$47,500–$51,000	20%
$25,500–$39,500	$51,000–$79,000	10%

Using health savings accounts

You can reduce your taxable income and sock away money for future healthcare expenses by taking advantage of a *health savings account* (HSA). In fact, HSAs can offer superior tax savings versus retirement accounts because in addition to providing up-front tax breaks on contributions and tax-free accumulation of investment earnings, you can also withdraw money from HSAs tax-free so long as the money is used for healthcare costs. No other retirement accounts offer this triple tax-free benefit.

Shifting some income

Income shifting, which has nothing to do with money laundering, is a more esoteric tax-reduction technique that's an option only to those who can control *when* they receive their income.

For example, suppose your employer tells you in late December that you're eligible for a bonus. You're offered the option to receive your bonus in either December or January. If you're pretty certain that you'll be in a higher tax bracket next year, you should choose to receive your bonus in December.

Or, suppose you run your own business and you think that you'll be in a lower tax bracket next year. Perhaps you plan to take time off to be with a newborn or take an extended trip. You can send out some invoices later in the year so your customers won't pay you until January, which falls in the next tax year.

Increasing Your Deductions

Deductions are amounts you subtract from your adjusted gross income before calculating the tax you owe. To make things more complicated, the IRS gives you two methods for determining your total deductions. The good news is that you get to pick the method that leads to greater deductions — and hence, lower taxes. This section explains your options.

Choosing standard or itemized deductions

The first method for figuring deductions requires no thinking or calculating. If you have a relatively uncomplicated financial life, taking the so-called *standard deduction* is generally the better option. With the tax reform bill implemented in 2018, more people are better off taking the standard deduction. And that is, in fact, what has been happening with nearly nine in ten taxpayers now taking the standard deduction (down from about two-thirds previously).

Single folks qualify for a $15,000 standard deduction, and married couples filing jointly get a $30,000 standard deduction in 2025. If you're 65 or older, or blind, you get a slightly higher standard deduction.

Itemizing your deductions on your tax return is the other method for determining your allowable deductions. This method is definitely more of a hassle, but if you can tally up more than the standard amounts noted in the preceding paragraph, itemizing will save you money. Use Schedule A of IRS Form 1040 to tally your itemized deductions.

TIP

Even if you take the standard deduction, take the time to peruse all the line items on Schedule A to familiarize yourself with the many legal itemized deductions. Figure out what's possible to deduct so you can make more-informed financial decisions year-round.

Purchasing real estate

When you buy a home, you can claim two big ongoing expenses of homeownership as deductions on Schedule A: your property taxes and the interest on your mortgage. You're allowed to claim mortgage interest deductions for a primary residence (where you actually live) and on a second home for mortgage debt totaling up to $750,000, which is down from the previous limit of $1 million (and a home equity loan of up to $100,000). You may be grandfathered under the higher $1 million limit if your mortgage was taken out before December 16, 2017, or if you had a home under contract by that date and closed on that purchase by April 1, 2018.

Before 2018, there was no limit on property tax deductions on Form 1040, Schedule A. Now, property taxes (combined with state and local income tax payments) are limited to a maximum $10,000 annual deduction.

Check out Chapter 6 for more on investing in real estate.

Trading consumer debt for mortgage debt

When you own real estate, you haven't borrowed the maximum, and you've run up high-interest consumer debt, you may be able to trade one debt for another. You may be able to save on interest charges by refinancing your mortgage or taking out a home equity loan and pulling out extra cash to pay off your credit card, auto loan, or other costly credit lines. You can usually borrow at a lower interest rate for a mortgage and get a tax deduction as a bonus, which lowers the effective borrowing cost further. Consumer debt, such as that on auto loans and credit cards, isn't tax-deductible.

WARNING

This strategy involves some danger. Borrowing against the equity in your home can be an addictive habit. I've seen cases where people run up significant consumer debt three or four times and then refinance their home the same number of times over the years to bail themselves out.

An appreciating home creates the illusion that excess spending isn't really costing you. But debt is debt, and all borrowed money ultimately has to be repaid (unless you file bankruptcy). In the long run, you wind up with greater mortgage debt, and paying it off takes a bigger bite out of your monthly income. Refinancing and establishing home equity lines cost you more in terms of loan application fees and other charges (points, appraisals, credit reports, and so on).

At a minimum, the continued expansion of your mortgage debt handicaps your ability to work toward other financial goals. In the worst case, easy access to borrowing encourages bad spending habits that can lead to bankruptcy or foreclosure on your debt-ridden home.

Contributing to charities

You can deduct contributions to charities if you itemize your deductions on Form 1040, Schedule A. Consider the following possibilities:

» Most people know that when they write a check for $50 to their favorite church or college, they can deduct it. *Note:* Make sure that you get a receipt for contributions of $250 or more.

» Many taxpayers overlook the fact that you can deduct expenses for work you do with charitable organizations. For example, when you go to a soup kitchen to help prepare and serve meals, you can deduct some of your transportation costs. Keep track of your driving mileage and other commuting expenses.

>> You can deduct the fair market value (which can be determined by looking at the price of similar merchandise in thrift stores) of donations of clothing, household appliances, furniture, and other goods to charities. (Some charities will drive to your home to pick up the stuff.) Find out whether organizations such as the Salvation Army, Goodwill, or others are interested in your donation. Just make sure that you keep some documentation — write up an itemized list and get it signed by the charity. Take pictures of your more valuable donations.

>> You can even donate securities and other investments to charity. In fact, donating an appreciated investment gives you a tax deduction for the full market value of the investment and eliminates your need to pay tax on the (unrealized) profit.

Remembering auto registration fees and state insurance

TIP

If you don't currently itemize, you may be surprised to discover that your state income taxes can be itemized. When you pay a fee to the state to register and license your car, you can itemize a portion of the expenditure as a deduction (on Schedule A, "State and Local Personal Property Taxes"). The IRS allows you to deduct the part of the fee that relates to the value of your car. The state organization that collects the fee should be able to tell you what portion of the fee is deductible. (Some states detail on the invoice what portion of the fee is tax-deductible.) There's a $10,000 annual federal income tax deduction limit on all deductible state and local taxes combined with property tax payments on your home.

Several states have state disability insurance funds. If you pay into these funds (check your W-2), you can deduct your payments as state and local income taxes on Line 5a of Schedule A. You may also claim a deduction on this line for payments you make into your state's unemployment compensation fund.

Deducting self-employment expenses

TIP

When you're self-employed, you can deduct a multitude of expenses from your income before calculating the tax you owe. If you buy a computer or office furniture, you can deduct those expenses. (Sometimes they need to be gradually deducted, or *depreciated,* over time.) Salaries for your employees, office supplies, rent or mortgage interest for your office space, and phone/communications expenses are also generally deductible.

Many self-employed folks don't take all the deductions they're eligible for. In some cases, people simply aren't aware of the wonderful world of deductions. Others are worried that large deductions will increase the risk of an audit. Spend some time finding out more about tax deductions; you'll be convinced that taking full advantage of your eligible deductions makes sense and saves you money.

Enlisting education tax breaks

The U.S. tax laws include numerous tax breaks for education-related expenditures. Here are the important tax-reduction opportunities you should know about for yourself and your kids if you have them:

>> **Tax deductions for college expenses:** You may take up to a $2,500 tax deduction on IRS Form 1040 for college costs as long as your modified adjusted gross income (AGI) is less than $85,000 for single taxpayers and less than $170,000 for married couples filing jointly. (*Note:* You may take a partial tax deduction if your AGI is between $85,000 and $100,000 for single taxpayers and between $170,000 and $200,000 for married couples filing jointly.)

>> **Tax-free investment earnings in special accounts:** Money invested in Section 529 plans is sheltered from taxation and is not taxed upon withdrawal as long as the money is used to pay for eligible education expenses. 529 plans allow you to sock away more than $200,000. However, funding such accounts may harm your kid's qualifications for financial aid.

>> **American Opportunity tax credit:** The American Opportunity credit provides tax relief to low- and moderate-income earners facing education costs. The full credit (up to $2,500 per student) is available to individuals whose modified adjusted gross income is $80,000 or less, or $160,000 or less for married couples filing jointly. The credit is phased out for single taxpayers above $90,000 and married couples filing jointly above $180,000. The credit can be claimed for expenses for the first four years of postsecondary education. You may be able to claim an American Opportunity tax credit

in the same year in which you receive a distribution from either an ESA or 529, but you can't use expenses paid with a distribution from either an ESA or 529 as the basis for the American Opportunity credit.

>> **Lifetime Learning tax credit:** The Lifetime Learning credit may be up to 20 percent of the first $10,000 of qualified educational expenses — up to $2,000 per taxpayer. For parents filing tax returns, only this credit or the American Opportunity tax credit may be claimed for each child per tax year. Single taxpayers' phaseout for being able to take this credit is at modified adjusted gross incomes (MAGIs) of $80,000 to $90,000. Other taxpayers' phaseout is from $160,000 to $180,000.

WARNING

The college financial aid system in this country assumes that the money you save outside tax-sheltered retirement accounts is available to pay educational expenses. As a result, families who save money outside instead of inside retirement accounts may qualify for far less "financial aid" than they otherwise would. Financial aid is actually a misnomer because what colleges and universities are doing is charging a different price to different families after analyzing their finances. So, when a college appears to be giving you money, what they're actually doing is reducing their inflated prices to a more reasonable level.

If you're affluent and have done a good job saving and investing money, colleges are generally going to charge you more. So in addition to normal income taxes, an extra financial aid "tax" is effectively exacted.

Making Tax-Wise Personal Finance Decisions

Taxes are a large and vital piece of your financial puzzle. The following list shows some of the ways that tax issues are involved in making sound financial decisions throughout the year:

>> **Spending:** The more you spend, the more taxes you'll pay for taxed purchases and for being less able to take advantage of the many benefits in the tax code that require you to have money to invest in the first place. For example, contrary

to the hucksters on late-night infomercials, you need money to purchase real estate, which offers many tax benefits (see Chapter 6). And because taxes are probably your largest or second biggest expenditure, a budget that overlooks tax-reduction strategies is likely doomed to fail. Unless you have wealthy, benevolent relatives, you may be stuck with a lifetime of working if you can't save money.

>> **Retirement accounts:** Taking advantage of retirement accounts can mean tens, perhaps even hundreds of thousands more dollars in your pocket come retirement time. Who says there are no free lunches? Check out Chapter 8.

>> **Investing:** Merely choosing investments that generate healthy rates of return isn't enough. What matters is not what you make but what you keep — after paying taxes. Understand and capitalize on the many tax breaks available to investors in stocks, bonds, mutual funds, exchange-traded funds, real estate, and your own business.

>> **Protecting your assets:** Some of your insurance decisions also affect the taxes you pay. You'd think that after a lifetime of tax payments, your heirs would be left alone when you pass on to the great beyond — wishful thinking. Estate planning can significantly reduce the taxes to be siphoned off from your estate. Peruse Chapter 9 to find out more about estate planning.

Taxes infiltrate many areas of your personal finances. Some people make important financial decisions without considering taxes (and other important variables). Conversely, in an obsession to minimize or avoid taxes, other people make decisions that are counterproductive to achieving their long-term personal and financial goals. Although this chapter shows you that taxes are an important component to factor into your major financial decisions, taxes should not drive or dictate the decisions you make.

Taming your taxes in non-retirement accounts

When you invest outside of tax-sheltered retirement accounts, the distributions on your money (for example, dividends) and realized gains when you sell are subject to taxation. So the non-retirement account investments that make sense for you depend (at least partly) on your tax situation.

If you have money to invest, or if you're considering selling current investments that you hold, taxes should factor into your decision. But tax considerations alone shouldn't dictate how and where you invest your money. You should also weigh investment choices, your desire and the necessity to take risk, personal likes and dislikes, and the number of years you plan to hold the investment.

Knowing what's taxed and when to worry

Interest you receive from bank accounts and corporate bonds is generally taxable. U.S. Treasury bonds pay interest that's state-tax-free. Municipal bonds, which state and local governments issue, pay interest that's federal-tax-free and also state-tax-free to residents in the state where the bond is issued.

Taxation on your *capital gains*, which is the *profit* (sales minus purchase price) on an investment, works under a unique system. Investments held less than one year generate *short-term capital gains*, which are taxed at your normal marginal rate.

Profits from investments that you hold longer than 12 months are *long-term capital gains*. These long-term gains cap at 20 percent, which is the rate that applies for those in the highest federal income tax brackets. This 20 percent long-term capital gains tax rate actually kicks in (for tax year 2025) at $533,400 of taxable income for single taxpayers and at $600,050 for married couples filing jointly.

The long-term capital gains tax rate is just 15 percent for everyone else, except for single taxpayers with taxable income up to $48,350 and married couples filing jointly with taxable income up to $96,700. For these folks, the long-term capital gains tax rate is 0 percent.

To help pay for the Affordable Care Act (Obamacare), taxpayers with total taxable income above $200,000 (single return) or $250,000 (joint return) from any source are also subject to a 3.8 percent extra tax on the lesser of the following:

>> Their net investment income, such as interest, dividends, and capital gains; net investment income excludes distributions from qualified retirement plans.

>> The amount, if any, by which their modified adjusted gross income (MAGI) exceeds the dollar thresholds; MAGI is adjusted gross income plus any tax-exempt interest income.

Devising tax-reduction strategies

Use these strategies to reduce the taxes you pay on investments that are exposed to taxation:

>> **Make use of retirement accounts and health savings accounts.** Most contributions to retirement accounts gain you an immediate tax break, and once they're inside the account, investment returns are sheltered from taxation, generally until withdrawal. Think of these as tax reduction accounts that can help you work toward achieving financial independence.

Similar to retirement accounts are health savings accounts (HSAs). With HSAs, you get a tax break on your contributions up-front; investment earnings compound without taxation over time; and there's no tax on withdrawal so long as the money is used to pay for health-related expenses (which enjoy a fairly broad list as delineated by the IRS).

>> **Consider tax-free money market funds and tax-free bond funds.** Tax-free investments yield less than comparable investments that produce taxable earnings, but because of the tax differences, the earnings from tax-free investments can end up being greater than what taxable investments leave you with. If you're in a high-enough tax bracket, you may find that you come out ahead with tax-free investments.

For a proper comparison, subtract what you'll pay in federal and state income taxes from the taxable investment income to see which investment nets you more.

TIP

>> **Invest in tax-friendly stock funds.** Mutual funds and exchange-traded funds that tend to trade less tend to produce lower capital gains distributions. For funds held outside tax-sheltered retirement accounts, this reduced trading effectively increases an investor's total rate of return. *Index funds* invest in a relatively static portfolio of securities, such as stocks and bonds. They don't attempt to beat the market; rather, they invest in the securities to mirror or match the performance of an underlying index. Although

index funds can't beat the market, the typical actively managed fund usually doesn't either, and index funds have several advantages over actively managed funds. See Chapter 3 to find out more about tax-friendly stock mutual funds, including some non-index funds and exchange-traded funds.

>> **Invest in small business and real estate.** The growth in value of business and real estate assets isn't taxed until you sell the asset. Even then, with investment real estate, you often can roll over the gain into another property as long as you comply with tax laws. Increases in value in small businesses can qualify for the more favorable longer-term capital gains tax rate and potentially for other tax breaks. However, the current income that small-business and real estate assets produce is taxed as ordinary income.

REMEMBER

Short-term capital gains (investments held one year or less) are taxed at your ordinary income tax rate. This fact is another reason why you shouldn't trade your investments quickly (within 12 months).

Avoiding taxing mistakes

Even if some parts of the tax system are hopelessly and unreasonably complicated, there's no reason why you can't learn from the mistakes of others to save yourself some money. With this goal in mind, this section details common tax blunders that people make when it comes to managing their money.

>> **Seeking advice after a major decision:** Too many people come across information and hire help after making a decision, even though seeking preventive help ahead of time generally is wiser and less costly. Before making any major financial decisions, educate yourself. This book can help answer many of your questions.

TIP

If you're going to hire a tax advisor to give advice, do so before making your decision(s). The wrong move when selling a piece of real estate or taking money from a retirement account can cost you thousands of dollars in taxes!

WARNING

>> **Failing to withhold enough taxes:** If you're self-employed or earn significant taxable income from investments outside retirement accounts, you need to be making estimated quarterly tax payments. Likewise, if, during the year,

you sell an investment at a profit, you may need to make a (higher) quarterly tax payment.

Not having a human resources department to withhold taxes from their pay as they earn it, some self-employed people dig themselves into a perpetual tax hole by failing to submit estimated quarterly tax payments. They get behind in their tax payments during their first year of self-employment and thereafter are always playing catch-up. People often don't discover that they "should've" paid more taxes during the year until after they complete their returns in the spring — or get penalty notices from the IRS and their states. Then they have to come up with sizable sums all at once. Don't be a "should've" victim.

To make quarterly tax payments, complete IRS Form 1040-ES, Estimated Tax for Individuals. This form and accompanying instructions explain how to calculate quarterly tax payments — which you can do through the IRS website or by mailing payment coupons with your check.

TIP

Although I — and the IRS — want you to keep your taxes current during the year, I don't want you to overpay. Some people have too much tax withheld during the year, and this overpayment can go on year after year. Although it may feel good to get a sizable refund check every spring, why should you loan your money to the government interest-free? When you work for an employer, you can complete a new W-4 to adjust your withholding. Turn the completed W-4 in to your employer. When you're self-employed, complete Form 1040-ES.

If you know that you'd otherwise spend the extra tax money that you're currently sending to the IRS, then this forced-savings strategy may have some value. But you can find other, better ways to make yourself save. You can set up all sorts of investments, such as mutual funds (see Chapter 3), to be funded by automatic contributions from your paychecks (or from a bank or investment account). Of course, if you happen to prefer to loan the IRS money — interest-free — go right ahead!

>> **Overlooking legitimate deductions:** Some taxpayers miss out on perfectly legal tax deductions because they just don't know about them. Ignorance is not bliss when it comes to your income taxes . . . it's costly. If you aren't going to take the time to discover the legitimate deductions available

to you, spring for the cost of a competent tax advisor at least once.

Fearing an audit, some taxpayers (and even some tax preparers) avoid taking deductions that they have every right to take. Unless you have something to hide, such behavior is foolish and costly. Remember that a certain number of returns are randomly audited every year, so even when you don't take every deduction to which you're legally entitled, you may nevertheless get audited. An hour or so with the IRS is not as bad as you may think. It may be worth the risk of claiming all the tax breaks to which you're entitled, especially when you consider the amounts you can save over the years.

>> **Passing up retirement accounts:** All the tax deductions and tax deferrals that come with accounts such as 401(k)s, 403(b)s, SEP-IRAs, and IRAs were put in the tax code to encourage you to save for retirement. So, why not take advantage of the benefits? See Chapter 8 to find out all about retirement accounts and why you should probably fund them.

>> **Ignoring tax considerations when investing:** Don't forget to consider the taxes due on profits from the sale of investments (except those in retirement accounts) when making decisions about what you sell and when you sell it. Your tax situation should also factor in what you invest outside retirement accounts. When you're in a relatively high tax bracket, you probably don't want investments that pay much in taxable distributions such as taxable interest, which only add to your tax burden. See the earlier "Taming your taxes in non-retirement accounts" section for details on the tax considerations of investing and which investments are tax-friendly for your situation.

>> **Not buying a home:** In the long run, owning a home should cost you less than renting. And because mortgage interest and property taxes may be partially deductible, the government, in effect, subsidizes the cost of home ownership.

Even if the government didn't help you with tax benefits when buying and owning a home, you'd still be better off owning throughout your adult life. If you rent instead, all your housing expenses are exposed to inflation, unless you have a great rent-controlled deal. So, owning your own abode makes good financial and tax sense. And don't let the lack of money for a down payment stand in your way — methods exist for buying real estate with little up-front money. See Chapter 6 to find out about real estate investing.

>> **Allowing your political views to distort your decision-making:** To be a successful investor and make sound financial decisions, try to leave your political beliefs out of it and be unemotional. Extreme changes rarely occur even when one party–rule occurs for a couple of years in Washington, D.C. It's often soon replaced by divided government, which leads to more incremental change and eventually a switch in power back to the current out-of-power party.

Ignoring the financial aid (tax) system: The college financial aid system in this country assumes that the money you save outside tax-sheltered retirement accounts is available to pay educational expenses. Refer to the section "Enlisting education tax breaks" for details about the college financial aid system and taxes.

>> **Neglecting the timing of events you can control:** The amount of tax you pay on certain transactions can vary, depending on the timing of events. If you're nearing retirement, for example, you may soon be in a lower tax bracket. To the extent possible, you should consider delaying and avoid claiming investment income until your overall income level drops, and you need to take as many deductions or losses as you can now while your income is still high. In addition to income shifting (see the "Shifting some income" section, earlier in this chapter), you can reduce taxes by bunching or shifting deductions.

When the total of your itemized deductions on Schedule A is lower than the standard deduction, you need to take the standard deduction. This itemized deduction total is worth checking each year, because you may have more deductions in some years than others, and you may occasionally be able to itemize.

When you can control the timing of payment of particular expenses that are eligible for itemizing, you can shift or bunch more of them into select years when you're more likely to have enough deductions to take advantage of itemizing. Suppose that because you don't have many itemized deductions this year, you use the standard deduction. Late in the year, however, you feel certain that you'll itemize next year, because you plan to buy a home and will therefore be able to claim significant mortgage interest and some property tax deductions. It makes sense, then, to shift and bunch as many deductible expenses as possible into next year. For example, if you're getting ready to make a tax-deductible donation of old clothes and household goods to charity, wait until January to do so.

In any tax year that you're sure you won't have enough deductions to be able to itemize, shift as many itemizable expenses as you can into the next tax year.

WARNING

Be careful when using your credit card to pay expenses. These expenses must be recognized for tax purposes in the year in which the charge was made on the card and not when you actually pay the credit card bill.

>> **Not using tax advisors effectively:** If your financial situation is complicated, going it alone and relying only on the IRS instructions to figure your taxes usually is a mistake. Many people find the IRS publications tedious and not geared toward highlighting opportunities for tax reductions. You can figure out taxes for yourself, or you can hire a tax advisor to figure them out for you. Doing nothing isn't an advisable option!

TIP

When you're overwhelmed by the complexity of particular financial decisions, get advice from tax and financial advisors who sell their time and nothing else. Protect yourself by checking references and clarifying what advice, analysis, and recommendations the advisor will provide for the fee charged. If your tax situation is complicated, you'll probably more than recoup a preparer's fee, as long as you take the time to hire a good advisor. The next section provides questions to ask when choosing a tax professional.

TIP

Remember that using a tax advisor is most beneficial when you face new tax questions or problems. If your tax situation remains complicated, or if you know that you'd do a worse job on your own, by all means keep using a tax preparer. But don't pay a big fee year after year to a tax advisor who simply plugs your numbers into the tax forms. If your situation is unchanging or isn't that complicated, consider hiring and paying someone to figure out your taxes one time. After that, go ahead and try completing your own tax return.

Hiring a tax professional

When you believe that your tax situation warrants outside help, be sure to educate yourself as much as possible beforehand. The more you know, the better able you'll be to evaluate the competence of someone you may hire. Following are questions to ask when you interview a tax preparer:

>> **What tax services do you offer?** Most tax advisors prepare tax returns. I use the term tax advisors because most tax folks do more than simply prepare returns. Many advisors can help you plan and file other important tax documents throughout the year. Some firms can also assist your small business with bookkeeping and other financial reporting, such as income statements and balance sheets. These services can be useful when your business is in the market for a loan or if you need to give clients or investors detailed information about your business.

>> **Do you have areas that you focus on?** Find out what expertise the tax advisor has in handling whatever unusual financial events you're dealing with this year — or whatever events you expect in future years. For example, if you need help completing an estate tax return for a deceased relative, ask how many of these types of returns the tax preparer has completed in the past year. About 15 percent of estate tax returns are audited, so you don't want a novice preparing one for you.

>> **What other services do you offer?** Ideally, you want to work with a professional who is 100 percent focused on taxes. I know it's difficult to imagine that some people choose to work at this full time, but they do — and lucky for you!

WARNING

A multitude of problems and conflicts of interest crop up when a person tries to prepare tax returns, sell investments, and appraise real estate — all at the same time. That advisor may not be fully competent or current in any of these areas.

By virtue of their backgrounds and training, some tax preparers also offer consulting and financial planning services for business owners and other individuals. Because they already know a great deal about your personal and tax situation, a competent tax professional may be able to help in these areas. Just make sure that this help is charged on an hourly consulting basis. Avoid tax advisors who sell financial products that pay them a commission — this situation inevitably creates conflicts of interest.

>> **Who will prepare my return?** If you talk to a solo practitioner, the answer to this question should be simple — the person you're talking to should prepare your return. But if your tax advisor has assistants and other employees, make sure that you know what level of involvement these different people will have in the preparation of your return.

It isn't necessarily bad if a junior-level person does the preliminary tax return preparation that your tax advisor will review and finalize. In fact, this procedure can save you money in tax-preparation fees if the firm bills you at a lower hourly rate for a junior-level person. Be wary of firms that charge you a high hourly rate for a senior tax advisor who then delegates most of the work to a junior-level person.

>> **How aggressive or conservative are you regarding tax strategies?** Assessing how aggressive a tax preparer is can be difficult. Start by asking what percentage of the tax preparer's clients get audited (see the next question). You can also ask the tax advisor for references from clients for whom the advisor helped unearth overlooked opportunities to reduce tax bills.

>> **What's your experience with audits?** As a benchmark, you need to know that less than 0.5 percent of all taxpayer returns are audited. For tax advisors working with a more affluent client base or small-business owners, expect a higher audit rate — somewhere in the neighborhood of 0.5 to 1 percent.

A tax preparer who has been in business for at least a couple of years will have gone through audits. Ask the preparer to explain their recent audits, what happened, and why. This explanation not only sheds light on a preparer's work with clients, but also on their ability to communicate in plain English. And if the tax preparer proudly claims no audited clients, be wary.

>> **How does your fee structure work?** Tax advisor fees, like attorney and financial planner fees, are all over the map — typically from $100 to $300+ per hour. Many preparers simply quote you a total fee for preparation of your tax return.

Ultimately, the tax advisor charges you for time, so you should ask what the hourly billing rate is. If the advisor balks at answering this question, try asking what their fee is for a one-hour consultation. You may want a tax advisor to work on this basis if you've prepared your return yourself and want it reviewed as a quality-control check. You also may seek an hourly fee if you're on top of your tax preparation in general but have some very specific questions about an unusual or one-time event, such as the sale of your business.

Clarify whether the preparer's set fee includes follow-up questions that you may have during the year, or if this fee covers IRS audits on the return. Some accountants include these functions in their set fee, but others charge for everything on an as-needed basis. The advantage of the all-inclusive fee is that it removes the psychological obstacle of your feeling that the meter's running every time you call with a question. The drawback can be that you pay for additional services (time) that you may not need or use.

» **What qualifies you to be a tax advisor?** Tax advisors come with a variety of backgrounds. The more tax and business experience they have, the better. Tax advisors can earn certifications such as CPAs and EAs. Although gaining credentials takes time and work, these certifications are no guarantee that you get quality, cost-effective tax assistance or that you won't be overcharged.

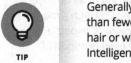

TIP

Generally speaking, more years of experience are better than fewer, but don't rule out a newer advisor who lacks gray hair or who hasn't yet slogged through thousands of returns. Intelligence and training can easily make up for less experience. Newer advisors also may charge less so they can build up their practices.

» **Do you carry liability insurance?** If a tax advisor makes a major mistake or gives poor advice, you can lose thousands of dollars. The greater your income, assets, and the importance of your financial decisions, the more financial harm that can be done. Your tax advisor needs to carry what's known as errors and omissions, or liability insurance. You can, of course, simply sue an uninsured advisor and hope the advisor has enough personal assets to cover a loss, but don't count on it. Besides, you'll have a much more difficult time getting due compensation that way!

You may also ask the advisor whether they have ever been sued and how the lawsuit turned out. It doesn't occur to most people to ask this type of question, so make sure that you tell your tax advisor that you're not out to strike it rich on a lawsuit! Another way to discover whether a tax advisor has gotten into hot water is by checking with appropriate professional organizations to which that preparer may belong. You can also check whether any complaints have been filed with your local Better Business Bureau (BBB), although this is far from a foolproof screening method. Most dissatisfied clients don't bother to register complaints with the BBB, and you should also know that the BBB is loath to retain complaints on file against companies who are members.

>> **Can you provide references of clients similar to me?** You need to know that the tax advisor has handled cases and problems like yours. For example, if you're a small-business owner, ask to speak with other small-business owners. But don't be overly impressed by tax advisors who claim that they work mainly with one occupational group, such as physicians. Although there's value in understanding the nuances of a profession, tax advisors are ultimately generalists — as are the tax laws.

Chapter **8**

Planning Financial Independence

This chapter provides the wealth-building wisdom you need to get the most out of planning for your future financial independence. In this chapter, you see how having a savings plan that works with all your competing financial goals is vital to successful retirement planning. I help you figure out how much money you need to save to achieve financial independence when you want. I also describe the types of retirement accounts that may be available to you and recommend how to prioritize retirement contributions and allocate funds.

Grasping the Keys to Successful Retirement Planning

Although you may like to consider other factors — such as your health, relationships with friends and family, and interests and activities — as more important than money, the bottom line is that money and your personal financial fitness are extra-important factors in your retirement lifestyle.

Getting caught up in planning the financial part of your future appears easy. After all, money is measurable, and so much revolves around the money component of retirement planning. So what can you do to successfully plan for retirement? You could simply work really hard and spend lots of time making as much money as possible. But what would be the point if you had little free time to enjoy yourself and others? Fortunately, you can implement the following strategies when planning for retirement.

Saving drives wealth

You may think a high income is key to having a prosperous retirement, but research shows that the best way to retirement bliss is to save. Research demonstrates that wealth accumulation is driven more by the choice to save (rather than spend) than it is by a person's income.

For example, professors Steven Venti and David Wise examined nearly 4,000 households across an array of income levels to challenge the notion that many households lacking high incomes don't earn enough money to both pay their bills and save at the same time.

Venti and Wise examined these households' current financial statuses and histories to explain the differences in their accumulations of assets. Their findings showed that the bulk of the differences among households ". . . must be attributed to differences in the amount that households choose to save. The differences in saving choices among households with similar lifetime earnings led to vastly different levels of asset accumulation by the time retirement age approaches."

It's not what you make but what you keep (save) that's important to building wealth. Of course, earning more *should* make it easier to save, but many folks allow their spending to increase with their incomes.

Keeping your balance

Most people have more than one goal when it comes to their money and personal situations. For example, suppose Ray, age 50, wants to scale back work to a part-time basis and spend more time traveling. He reasons, "I don't want to wait until my 70s, because what if my health isn't great or I don't make it!" But Ray also wants to help his adult children with some of the costs of graduate school and possibly with buying their first homes.

Ray's situation — of having multiple goals competing for limited dollars — is often the norm. Thus, a theme discussed throughout this book is how to trade off competing goals, which requires personal considerations and balance in one's life.

Unless you have really deep pockets and modest goals, you need to prioritize and develop price tags for each of your goals.

Understanding that planning is a process

The Aircraft Owners and Pilots Association has a slogan: "A good pilot is always learning." Likewise, to have a good retirement, you should view planning as an ongoing activity, not a one-time endeavor. Financial planning is a process. Too many people develop financial plans and then think they're finished. Taking this route is a good way to run into unpleasant surprises in the future.

A plan is based on assumptions and forecasts. However, no plan — no matter how carefully it's developed — gets all the assumptions and forecasts correct. Even your best, most careful guesses may miss the mark. So every few years, you should review and update your plan.

As you're reviewing, assess how much reality differed from your assumptions. Sometimes, you'll be pleasantly surprised. Your portfolio may earn more than you expected, or you may spend less than you estimated.

Other times, the review won't be as pleasant. The markets may have dragged down your portfolio returns. Or your spending may have exceeded your estimates. In either case, you aren't reaching your goals.

Even if you do meet the mark in most instances, you still are never really done planning and revising. You're bound to experience changes in your life, the economy, the financial markets, tax law, and other areas. You may come across new opportunities that weren't available a few years ago or that weren't right for you then but make sense now. You need to continually adapt your plan to these changes. You may need to adjust your spending or change your investment portfolio.

You don't have to be obsessive. Daily, or even quarterly, changes in your portfolio that are different from the plan aren't a reason to go back to the drawing board. But every year or so (or when you have a major change in your personal situation), take a fresh look. Review the plan and your progress. Figure out what went right and what went wrong. Decide whether your goals or situation have changed and whether any adjustments are needed. Finally, implement the new plan and enjoy life. After all, that's what the money is for.

Figuring Out When You Can Stop Punching the Clock

Retiring sounds so appealing when you've had a frustrating stretch at a job you're not particularly enjoying. But some folks really enjoy working and aren't eager to have wide-open daily schedules day after day, week after week. Deciding when to retire and what to do in retirement is an intensely personal decision. For sure, there are many financial and personal considerations and questions.

Even when you're healthy, the job market may not be. Your employer could suffer financial hardship and reduce its workforce. You may lose your job with little notice and few benefits. Or maybe you'll be lucky enough to retire early (even though it's unplanned) because your employer offers you a buy-out package that's too good to turn down.

Ideally, when caught in one of these situations, you would obtain another job and continue it until your planned retirement age. Unfortunately, events may not unfold that way. The economy, the job market, and your age can work against you. Finding another job, at a compensation level you're willing to work for, may not be possible.

Even when you leave a full-time career voluntarily, you may plan to work part-time for a few years. Or you may assume that if the first years of retirement are more expensive than planned, you can return to work at least part-time. Yet a part-time job you assumed would be easy to find may not be available at all or may be available at a much lower level of pay than you expected.

Knowing How Much You Really Need for Retirement

If you're like most people, you need less money to live on in retirement than during your working years. That's because in retirement most people don't need to save any of their income and many of their work-related expenses (commuting, work clothes, and such) go away or greatly decrease. With less income, most retirees find they pay less in taxes, too.

On the flip side, some categories of expenses may go up in retirement. With more free time on your hands, you may spend more on entertainment, restaurants, and travel. The costs for prescription drugs and other medical expenses also can begin to add up.

To help figure out how much money you need, keep the following statistics in mind. Studies have shown that retirees typically spend 65 to 80 percent of their pre-retirement income during their retirement years. Folks at the lower end of this range typically

» Save a large portion of their annual earnings during their working years

» Don't have a mortgage or any other debt in retirement

» Are higher-income earners who don't anticipate leading a lifestyle in retirement that's reflective of their current high income

Those who spend at the higher end of the range tend to have the following characteristics:

» Save little or none of their annual earnings before retirement

» Still have a significant mortgage or growing rent to pay in retirement

>> Need nearly all current income to meet their current lifestyle

>> Have expensive hobbies that they have more time to pursue

TIP

Numerous useful retirement planning analytic tools are available that you can use to assess where you currently stand in terms of saving for retirement. Among the various mass market website retirement tools, I really like T. Rowe Price's (www.troweprice.com/usis/advice/tools/retirement-income-calculator) and Vanguard's (investor.vanguard.com/calculator-tools/retirement-income-calculator/).

REMEMBER

I can't offer a definitive answer as to how much you personally may need to have for your retirement. Just make sure you carefully look at all your expenses and figure out how they may change.

Eyeing the components of your retirement plan

In order to meet your retirement goals, you need a firm grasp of what resources are available to help you. In addition to government benefits such as Social Security, company-provided pensions and personal investments round out most people's retirement income sources. This section takes a closer look at these elements.

Social Security retirement benefits

Social Security is intended to provide a subsistence/modest level of income in retirement for basic living necessities such as food, shelter, and clothing. However, Social Security wasn't designed to be a retiree's sole source of income. When planning for retirement, you'll likely need to supplement your expected Social Security benefits with personal savings, investments, and company pension benefits. If you're a high-income earner, you particularly need to supplement your income — unless, of course, you're willing to live well beneath your pre-retirement income.

If you're still working, you can estimate your Social Security retirement benefits by looking at your most recent Social Security benefits summary at www.ssa.gov/myaccount/ or by calling 800-772-1213 and requesting Form SSA-7004 ("Request for Social Security Statement"). Setting up a "my Social Security" account on the Social Security website lets you obtain updated benefits estimates, verify your earnings, and take other actions.

By reviewing your Social Security account, you can see how much in Social Security benefits you've already earned and review how the Social Security Administration (SSA) determines these numbers. With this information, you can better plan for your retirement and make important retirement planning decisions.

TIP

If you want to delve into different scenarios for your Social Security benefits, use the SSA's online Retirement Estimator at www.ssa.gov/benefits/retirement/estimator.html.

Pensions

When putting together your retirement plan, you also want to consider any pensions you have available to you. Also known as a *defined benefit plan,* a company pension plan is one that your employer actually is contributing to and investing money in to fund your future pension payments.

If your current or previous employers have a pension plan and you may have accumulated benefits, request a copy of each plan's benefit description and a recent statement of your earned benefits. (When you get to crunching the numbers for your retirement plan, you need your pension benefit statements.)

Based on your years of service, your benefits statement will show you how much of a benefit you've earned. Your current employer's statement or the person or department that works with benefits may also be able to show you how your pension benefits will increase based on working until a certain future age.

Investments

The many types of investments you may have are an important component of your retirement plan. These investments may come in various forms, such as bank accounts, brokerage accounts, mutual fund accounts, and so on. Your investments may or may not be in retirement accounts. Even if they aren't, they still can be earmarked to help with your retirement.

Take an inventory of your savings and investments by gathering recent copies of your statements (or checking balances online if you've gone paperless) from the following types of accounts or investment options:

>> Bank accounts — checking (especially if it holds excess savings), savings, CDs, and so on

>> IRA accounts

>> Taxable accounts at brokers and mutual funds

>> Employer retirement accounts, including

- Profit-sharing plans

- Employee stock ownership plans (ESOPs)

- 401(k)s, 403(b)s, and so forth

>> Investment real estate

You will use this inventory of your current assets in the "Crunching the numbers" section to determine where you stand regarding retirement planning.

Your home's equity

If you've owned a home over the years and it has a decent amount of *equity* in it (the difference between its market value and the mortgage debt owed on it), you can tap into that equity to provide for your retirement. In order to tap into your home's equity, you have two primary options:

>> **You can sell your home.** After you sell your home, you can either buy a less costly one or rent.

>> **You can take out a reverse mortgage.** With a *reverse mortgage,* you continue to live in your home and draw income against your home, which is accumulated as a debt balance to be paid once the home is sold.

If you're pretty certain you'd like to tap your home's equity to help with retirement, consider how much equity you would use.

Crunching the numbers

Numerous mass market website tools exist and focus on retirement planning. Many investment firms offer these to lure you to their websites. Some require you to register, whereas others can be accessed as a "guest." Such tools walk you through the calculations needed to figure how much you should be saving to reach your retirement goal.

The assumptions that you plug into these calculators are really important, so here's a review of the key ones:

>> **Asset allocation:** Enter your current *allocation* (the portion invested in stocks versus bonds). You'll also typically select an allocation for after you're retired. Most such calculators don't include real estate as a possible asset. If you own real estate as an investment, you should treat those assets as a stock-like investment, since they have similar long-term risk and return characteristics. (Calculate your equity in investment real estate, which is the difference between a property's current market value and mortgage debt on that property.)

>> **Age of retirement:** Plug in your preferred age of retirement, within reason, of course. There's no point plugging in a dream number like "I'd like to retire by age 45, but I know the only way I can do that is to win the lottery!" Depending on how the analysis works out, you can always go back and plug in a different age.

>> **Include Social Security:** Some calculators ask whether you want to include expected Social Security benefits. I'd rather that they didn't pose this question at all, because you definitely should include your Social Security benefits in the calculations. Based on your current income, the calculator will automatically plug in your estimated benefits. So long as your income hasn't changed or won't change dramatically, using the calculator's estimated number should be fine. Alternatively, you can use your personal information that you can access on the Social Security website at www.ssa.gov.

Many calculators allow you to make adjustments such as to your desired age of retirement, rate of savings, and to what age you'd like your savings to last. So, for example, if the analysis shows that you have much more than enough to retire by age 65, try plugging in, say, age 62 and voilà, the calculator quickly shows you how the numbers change.

TIP

Among the mass market website retirement planning tools and booklets, I like T. Rowe Price's. Visit www.troweprice.com for the online version or call 800-638-5660 for the work booklets. The T. Rowe Price web-based Retirement Income Calculator (www3.troweprice.com/ric/ricweb/public/ric.do) is a user-friendly tool, and the website says it takes about 10 minutes to complete. If you're organized and have your documents handy, you may cruise through it that quickly, but otherwise you'll more than likely need 20 to 30 minutes.

Making the numbers work

After you crunch the numbers, you may discover you need to save at a rate that isn't doable. Don't despair. You have the following options to lessen the depressingly high savings you apparently need:

>> **Boost your investment returns.** Reduce your taxes while investing: While you're still working, be sure to take advantage of retirement savings accounts, especially when you can gain free matching money from your employer or you're eligible for the special tax credit from the government. When investing money outside of retirement accounts, take care to minimize taxes. For more on investing strategies, see Chapter 3.

>> **Work (a little) more.** Extend the number of years you're willing to work or consider working part-time for a few years past the age you were expecting to stop working.

>> **Reduce your spending.** The more you spend today, the more years you'll have to work in order to meet your savings goal.

>> **Use your home's equity.** If you didn't factor using some of your home's equity into your retirement nest egg, consider doing so. Some people are willing to trade down into a less costly property in retirement. You also can take a reverse mortgage to tap some of your current home's equity. See more about home equity and reverse mortgages in the earlier section "Your home's equity."

Dealing with excess money

If you find yourself with extra money, the good news is that you can have peace of mind and more confidence about achieving your desired standard of living during retirement. In this situation, consider taking either of the following actions:

>> **Enhance your retirement.** Don't be afraid to enjoy yourself. While you're still healthy, travel, eat out, take some classes, and do whatever else floats your boat (within reason, of course). Remember that come the end of your life, you can't take your money with you.

>> **Earmark a portion of your assets for your beneficiaries.** You may want to leave something for your family members as well as other beneficiaries, such as your place of worship and charities. If so, you need to determine the approximate dollar amount for each of the beneficiaries.

REMEMBER

Of course, life can throw you unexpected curveballs that may cause you to incur higher-than-expected expenses. But if you're always preparing for rainy day after rainy day, you may lead a miserly, unenjoyable retirement.

Chariots of Freedom: Your Retirement Accounts

A *retirement account* is simply a shell or shield that keeps the federal, state, and local governments from taxing your investment earnings each year. You choose what investments you want to hold inside your retirement account shell.

If you earn employment income (or receive alimony), you have options for putting money away in a retirement account that compounds without taxation until you withdraw the money. In most cases, your contributions to these retirement accounts are tax-deductible.

The following list describes the types of retirement account that are suited to various situations.

>> **Company-based retirement plans:** Larger for-profit companies generally offer their employees a *401(k)* plan, which typically allows saving up to $23,500 per year (for tax year 2025). Many nonprofit organizations offer

their employees similar plans, known as *403(b)* plans. Contributions to both traditional 401(k) and 403(b) plans are deductible on both your federal and state taxes in the year that you make them. Employees of nonprofit organizations can generally contribute up to 20 percent or $23,500 of their salaries, whichever is less.

TIP

There's a benefit in addition to the up-front and ongoing tax benefits of these retirement savings plans: Some employers match your contributions. Of course, the challenge for many people is to reduce their spending enough to be able to sock away these kinds of contributions.

Some employers are offering a Roth 401(k) account, which, like a Roth IRA (discussed in the next section), offers employees the ability to contribute on an after-tax basis. Withdrawals from such accounts generally aren't taxed in retirement.

If you're self-employed, you can establish your own retirement savings plans for yourself and any employees you have. *Simplified Employee Pension-Individual Retirement Accounts* (SEP-IRA) allow you to put away up to 20 percent of your self-employment income up to an annual maximum of $70,000 (for tax year 2025).

Individual Retirement Accounts: If you work for a company that doesn't offer a retirement savings plan, or if you've exhausted contributions to your company's plan, consider an *Individual Retirement Account* (IRA). Anyone who earns employment income or receives alimony may contribute up to $7,000 annually to an IRA (or the amount of your employment income or alimony income, if it's less than $7,000 in a year). A nonworking spouse may contribute up to $7,000 annually to a spousal IRA.

Your contributions to an IRA may or may not be tax-deductible. For tax year 2025, if you're single and your adjusted gross income is $77,000 or less for the year, you can deduct your full IRA contribution. If you're married and you file your taxes jointly, you're entitled to a full IRA deduction if your AGI is $123,000 per year or less.

TIP

If you can't deduct your contribution to a standard IRA account, consider making a contribution to a nondeductible IRA account called the *Roth IRA*. Single taxpayers with an AGI less than $150,000 and joint filers with an AGI less than

$236,000 can contribute up to $7,000 per year to a Roth IRA. Although the contribution isn't deductible, earnings inside the account are shielded from taxes, and unlike withdrawals from a standard IRA, qualified withdrawals from a Roth IRA account are free from income tax.

TIP

Should you be earning a high enough income that you can't fund a Roth IRA, there's an indirect "backdoor" way to fund a Roth IRA. First, you contribute to a regular IRA as a nondeductible contribution. Then, you can convert your regular IRA contribution into a Roth IRA. Please note that this so-called backdoor method generally only makes sense if you don't have other money already invested in a regular IRA because in that case, you can't simply withdraw your most recent contribution and not owe any tax.

You may invest the money in your IRA or self-employed plan retirement account (such as a SEP-IRA) in stocks, bonds, mutual funds, and some other common investments, including bank accounts. Mutual funds (offered in most employer-based plans) and exchange-traded funds (ETFs) are ideal choices because they offer diversification and professional management. See Chapter 3 for more on mutual funds and ETFs.

>> **Annuities: Maxing out your retirement savings:** What if you have so much cash sitting around that after maxing out your contributions to retirement accounts, including your IRA, you still want to sock more away into a tax-advantaged account? Enter the annuity. *Annuities* are contracts that insurance companies back. If you, the investor (annuity holder), should die during the so-called accumulation phase (that is, before receiving payments from the annuity), your designated beneficiary is guaranteed reimbursement of the amount of your original investment.

Annuities, like IRAs, allow your capital to grow and compound tax-deferred. You defer taxes until you withdraw the money. Unlike an IRA, which has an annual contribution limit of a few thousand dollars, an annuity allows you to deposit as much as you want in any year — even millions of dollars, if you've got millions! As with a Roth IRA, however, you get no up-front tax deduction for your contributions.

Because annuity contributions aren't tax-deductible, and because annuities carry higher annual operating fees to pay for the small amount of insurance that comes with them, don't consider contributing to one until you've fully exhausted your other retirement account investing options. Because of their higher annual expenses, annuities generally make sense only if you won't need the money for 15 or more years.

Getting the Most from Your Retirement Accounts

With good reason, people are concerned about placing their retirement account money in investments that can decline in value. You may feel that you're gambling with dollars intended for the security of your golden years.

Most working folks need to make their money work hard in order for it to grow fast enough to provide this security. This need involves taking some risk; you have no way around it. Luckily, if you have 15 to 20 years or more before you need to draw on the bulk of your retirement account assets, time is on your side. As long as the value of your investments has time to recover, what's the big deal if some of your investments drop a bit over a year or two? The more years you have before you're going to retire, the greater your ability to take risk.

Think of your retirement accounts as part of your overall plan to generate retirement income. Then allocate different types of investments between your tax-deferred retirement accounts and other taxable investment accounts to get the maximum benefit of tax deferral. This section helps you determine how to distribute your money in retirement plans. Chapter 4 can help you decide how to divide your money among different nonretirement investment options based on your time frame and risk tolerance.

Prioritizing retirement contributions

When you have access to various retirement accounts, prioritize which account you're going to use first by determining how much each gives you in return. Your first contributions should be to employer-based plans that match your contributions. After that, you should generally contribute to any other employer or self-employed plans that allow tax-deductible contributions. After you contribute to these tax-deductible plans (or if you don't have access to such plans), consider an IRA. If you max out on contributions to an IRA or you don't have this choice because you lack employment income, consider an annuity (I cover annuities earlier in this chapter, in the section "Chariots of Freedom: Your Retirement Accounts").

There are, of course, exceptions to these generalizations. As I emphasize throughout this book, you need to be mindful of your competing financial goals when determining whether funding retirement accounts (or any other financial move) makes sense.

Setting up a retirement account

Investments and account types are different issues. People sometimes get confused when discussing the investments they make in retirement accounts — especially people who have a retirement account, such as an IRA, at a bank. They don't realize that you can have your IRA at a variety of financial institutions (for example, a mutual-fund company or investment brokerage firm). At each financial institution, you can choose among the firm's investment options for putting your IRA money to work.

No-load, or commission-free, mutual-fund and discount brokerage firms are your best bets for establishing a retirement account. For more specifics, see my recommendations throughout the remainder of this chapter.

Allocating money with employer-selected options

In some company-sponsored plans, such as 401(k)s, you're limited to the predetermined investment options your employer offers. In the following sections, I discuss common investment options for 401(k) plans in order of increasing risk and, hence, likely return. Then I follow with examples for how to allocate your money across the different types of common employer retirement plan options.

Money market/savings accounts

For regular contributions that come out of your paycheck, the money-market or savings account option makes little sense. Some people who are skittish about the stock and bond markets are attracted to money-market and savings accounts because they can't drop in value. However, the returns are low — so low that you have a notable risk that your investment will not stay ahead of, or even keep up with, inflation and taxes (which are due upon withdrawal of your money from the retirement account).

Don't be tempted to use a money-market fund as a parking place until you think stocks and bonds are cheap. In the long run, you won't be doing yourself any favors. As I discuss in Chapter 4, timing your investments to attempt to catch the lows and avoid the peaks isn't possible.

You may need to keep money in the money-market investment option if you use the borrowing feature that some retirement plans allow. Check with your employee benefits department for more details. After you retire, you may also want to use a money-market account to hold money you expect to withdraw and spend within a year or so.

Bond mutual funds

Bond mutual funds (which I describe in Chapter 3) invest in a mixture of typically high-quality bonds. Bonds pay a higher rate of interest or dividends than money funds. Depending on whether your plan's option is a short-term, intermediate-term, or long-term fund (maybe you have more than one type), the bond fund's current yield is probably a percent or two higher than the money-market fund's yield. (*Note:* During certain time periods, the yield difference may be more, whereas during other time periods, it may be less.)

Bond funds carry higher yields than money-market funds, but they also carry greater risk because their value can fall if interest rates increase. However, bonds tend to be more stable in value over the shorter term (such as a few years) than stocks.

Aggressive, younger investors should keep a minimum amount of money in bond funds. Older folks who want to invest conservatively can place more money in bonds (see the asset allocation discussion in Chapter 4).

Guaranteed-investment contracts (GICs)

Guaranteed-investment contracts (GICs) are backed by an insurance company, and they typically quote you a rate of return projected one or a few years forward. Thus, you don't have the uncertainty that you normally face with bond or stock investments (unless, of course, the insurance company fails).

The attraction of these investments is that your account value doesn't fluctuate (at least, not that you can see). Insurers normally invest your money mostly in bonds and maybe a bit in stocks. The difference between what these investments generate for the insurer and what they pay in interest to GIC investors is profit to the insurer. A GIC's yield is usually comparable to that of a bond fund.

TIP

For people who hit the eject button the moment a bond fund slides a bit in value, GICs are soothing to the nerves. And they're certainly higher yielding than a money-market or savings account.

Like bonds, however, GICs don't give you the opportunity for much long-term growth above the rate of inflation. Over the long haul, you can expect to earn a better return in a mixture of bond and stock investments. In GICs, you pay for the peace of mind of a guaranteed return with lower long-term returns.

GICs also have another minor drawback: Insurance companies, unlike mutual funds, can and do fail, putting GIC investment dollars at risk. Some employers' retirement plans have been burned by insurance company failures.

Balanced/target date mutual funds

Balanced mutual funds invest primarily in a mixture of stocks and bonds. This one-stop-shopping concept makes investing easier and reduces fluctuations in the value of your investments — funds investing exclusively in stocks or in bonds make for a rougher ride. These funds are solid options and, in fact, can be used for a significant portion of your retirement plan contributions. See Chapter 3 to find out more about balanced funds.

Some fund companies offer funds of funds known as a *target date mutual fund*. These funds include a mixture of stocks and bonds;

the mix gets gradually more conservative (less risky) over the years as a person nears retirement.

Stock mutual funds

Stock mutual funds invest in stocks, which often provide greater long-term growth potential but also wider fluctuations in value from year to year. Some companies offer a number of different stock funds, including funds that invest internationally or globally. Unless you plan to borrow against your funds to purchase a home (if your plan allows), you should have a healthy helping of stock funds. See Chapter 3 for an explanation of the different types of stock funds as well as for details on how to evaluate a stock fund.

Stock in the company you work for

WARNING

Some companies offer employees the option of investing in the company's stock. I generally advocate avoiding this option for the simple reason that your future income and other employee benefits are already riding on the success of the company. If the company hits the skids, you may lose your job and your benefits. You certainly don't want the value of your retirement account to depend on the same factors.

In the early 2000s, you may have heard all the hubbub about companies such as Enron going under and employees losing piles of money in their retirement savings plans. Enron's bankruptcy in and of itself shouldn't have caused direct problems in Enron's 401(k) plan. The problem was that Enron required employees to hold substantial amounts of Enron company stock. Thus, when the company tanked, employees lost their jobs *and* their retirement savings balances invested in their company's stock.

Thanks to the Employee Retirement Income Security Act (ERISA), companies are no longer allowed to force employees to hold retirement plan money in company stock. Specifically, ERISA rules require companies to offer prudent and adequately diversified investments within their retirement savings plans. An option to invest in the employer's stock can be offered, but investing in the stock is now strictly optional, and it must be one of numerous investment options offered to employees.

If you think that your company has its act together and the stock is a good buy, investing a portion of your retirement account is fine — but no more than 20 to 25 percent. Now, if your company is on the verge of hitting it big and the stock is soon to soar, you'll of course be kicking yourself for not putting more of your money into the company's stock. But when you place a big bet on your company's stock, be prepared to suffer the consequences if the stock tanks. Don't forget that lots of smart investors track companies' prospects, so odds are that the current value of your company's stock is reasonably fair.

TIP

Some employers offer employees an additional option to buy company stock outside a tax-deferred retirement plan at a discount, sometimes as much as 15 percent when compared to its current market value. If your company offers a discount on its stock, take advantage of it. When you sell the stock, you'll usually be able to lock in a decent profit over your purchase price.

Some asset allocation examples

Table 8-1 shows a couple examples of how people in different employer plans may choose to allocate their 401(k) investments among the plan's investment options.

TABLE 8-1 Allocating 401(k) Investments

	25-Year-Old, Aggressive Risk Investor	45-Year-Old, Moderate Risk Investor	60-Year-Old, Moderate Risk Investor
Bond fund	0%	35%	50%
Balanced fund (50% stock/50% bond)	10%	0%	0%
Blue-chip/larger company stock fund(s)	30–40%	20–25%	25%
Smaller company stock fund(s)	20–25%	15–20%	10%
International stock fund(s)	25–35%	20–25%	15%

Allocating money in plans you design

With self-employed plans (such as SEP-IRAs and self-employed 401(k)s), certain 403(b) plans for nonprofit employees, and IRAs, you may select the investment options as well as the allocation of money among them. In the sections that follow, I give some specific recipes that you may find useful for investing at some of the premier investment companies.

To establish your retirement account at one of these firms, investment firms provide downloadable account applications on their websites, and some allow you to complete the application online. Alternatively, you can call the company's toll-free number and ask the representative to mail you an account application for the type of account (for example, SEP-IRA, 403(b), and so on) you want to set up.

Note: In the examples, I make recommendations for a conservative portfolio and an aggressive portfolio for each firm. I use the terms *conservative* and *aggressive* in a relative sense. Because some of the funds I recommend don't maintain fixed percentages of their different types of investments, the actual percentage of stocks and bonds that you end up with may vary slightly from the targeted percentages. Don't sweat it.

TIP

Where you have more than one fund choice, you can pick one or split the suggested percentage among them. If you don't have enough money today to divvy up your portfolio as I suggest, you can achieve the desired split over time as you add more money to your retirement accounts.

Vanguard

Vanguard (phone 877-662-7447; website www.vanguard.com) is a mutual-fund and exchange-traded fund powerhouse, and it also operates a discount brokerage division. It's the largest no-load fund company, and it consistently has the lowest operating expenses in the business. Historically, Vanguard's funds have shown excellent performance when compared to those of the company's peers, especially among conservatively managed bond and stock funds.

A CONSERVATIVE PORTFOLIO WITH 50 PERCENT STOCKS, 50 PERCENT BONDS

If you don't want to risk too much, try this:

>> Vanguard Total Bond Market Index — 25 percent
>> Vanguard Star (balanced fund of funds) — 60 percent
>> Vanguard International Value *and/or* Vanguard Total International Stock Index — 15 percent

AN AGGRESSIVE PORTFOLIO WITH 80 PERCENT STOCKS, 20 PERCENT BONDS

If you want to be aggressive, try this:

>> Vanguard Star (fund of funds) — 50 percent
>> Vanguard Total Stock Market Index — 30 percent
>> Vanguard International Value *and/or* Vanguard Total International Stock Index — 20 percent

Or you can place 100 percent in Vanguard LifeStrategy Growth (fund of funds).

Fidelity

Fidelity Investments (phone 800-343-3548; website www.fidelity.com) is a large provider of funds, and it operates a brokerage division. However, some Fidelity funds assess sales charges (no such funds are recommended in the sections that follow).

A CONSERVATIVE PORTFOLIO WITH 50 PERCENT STOCKS, 50 PERCENT BONDS

If you want to maintain a conservative portfolio, try this:

>> Fidelity Puritan (balanced fund) — 50 percent
>> Dodge & Cox Balanced — 50 percent

AN AGGRESSIVE PORTFOLIO WITH 80 PERCENT STOCKS, 20 PERCENT BONDS

If you want to maintain an aggressive portfolio, try this:

>> Fidelity Puritan (balanced fund) — 35 percent

>> Primecap Odyssey Growth — 25 percent

>> Fidelity Low-Priced Stock — 20 percent

>> Vanguard Total International Stock Index *and/or* Dodge & Cox International Stock — 20 percent

Discount brokers

A brokerage account can allow you centralized, one-stop shopping and the ability to hold funds from a variety of leading fund companies. Some funds are available without transaction fees, although some of the better funds require you to pay a small transaction fee when you buy funds through a broker. The reason: The brokerage firm is an intermediary between you and the fund companies. You have to weigh the convenience of being able to buy and hold funds from multiple fund companies in a single account versus the lower cost of buying funds directly from their providers. A $20 to $30 transaction fee can gobble a sizable chunk of what you have to invest, especially if you're investing smaller amounts.

Among brokerage firms or brokerage divisions of mutual-fund companies, for breadth of fund offerings and competitive pricing, I like Fidelity (phone 800-343-3548; website www.fidelity.com), Schwab (phone 800-435-4000; website www.schwab.com), T. Rowe Price (phone 800-225-5132; website www.troweprice.com), and Vanguard (phone 877-662-7447; website www.vanguard.com).

A CONSERVATIVE PORTFOLIO WITH 50 PERCENT STOCKS, 50 PERCENT BONDS

If you want to set up a conservative portfolio, try this:

>> Vanguard Short-Term Investment-Grade — 20 percent

>> Dodge & Cox Income — 20 percent

>> Dodge & Cox Balanced *and/or* Vanguard Wellington — 20 percent

>> T. Rowe Price Spectrum Growth (global stock fund of funds) — 30 percent

>> Dodge & Cox International *and/or* Vanguard Total International Stock Index — 10 percent

AN AGGRESSIVE PORTFOLIO WITH 80 PERCENT STOCKS, 20 PERCENT BONDS

If you want to set up an aggressive portfolio, try this:

>> Vanguard Total Bond Market Index — 20 percent

>> Vanguard Total Stock Market Index *and/or* Dodge & Cox Stock — 50 percent

>> Dodge & Cox International *and/or* Vanguard International Growth *and/or* Vanguard Total International Stock — 30 percent

Chapter **9**

Leaving a Legacy

An estate plan is an essential part of life because it determines what happens to your assets after you die and often how your assets are managed and you are cared for while you're alive but in need of assistance. An estate plan isn't simply a will or life insurance policy. And estate planning involves more than avoiding taxes. You need an estate plan even if your estate isn't valuable enough to be hit with estate taxes.

In this chapter, I define estate planning and review the basic elements of such a plan. I discuss how to go about developing a plan and how to work with an estate planning professional. Then I discuss wills, trusts, probate, taxes, and other estate planning subjects in more detail.

Understanding Estate Planning

Estate planning is the process of planning for the transfer of ownership of your assets to the recipients of your choice in the most efficient way possible — minimizing the taxes, other expenses, and time involved. The recipients may include your spouse, significant other, children, grandchildren, other loved ones, and charity.

A good estate plan ensures that your estate has enough cash to pay immediate (such as burial) and ongoing expenses, that any trusts you create are properly managed, and that your assets are managed and sold competently. Another feature of an estate plan is the designation of who will manage your assets, pay your bills, and make medical decisions if you're unable.

From a big-picture standpoint, the estate planning process has two important steps: deciding on your goals and deciding which legal tools to use to accomplish those goals.

However, estate planning isn't quite so simple. Here are the more detailed steps of the process:

1. List all your assets and debts.

Be sure to include all assets. The estate tax broadly defines assets. *Assets* include not only property you own (or partly own) but also rights you have such as in trusts, annuities, pensions, and life insurance.

Your list of *debts* (your legal obligations to pay money or property to others) is also important. Heirs inherit only *net assets* (gross assets less debts and other liabilities), and the estate won't be processed through probate until debts are paid. So, an estate plan must include a debt payment plan.

TIP

The more work you do to compile a complete list of assets and liabilities and prepare other information, the less your estate plan will cost. Check out the later section "Answering Key Questions to Gather Critical Information" to help you after you create your list and before you meet with your estate planner.

2. Prepare an income statement.

An *income statement* (also called a *cash flow statement*) is a list of the income and expenses you expect during the current year. If you prepare a monthly or annual budget, you already have this. It can be as formal or informal as you like. Its purpose is to give your estate planner and executor a clear picture of your cash inflows and outflows. Preparing this type of statement can help you develop a plan for the estate to pay bills and debts.

3. **Decide how you want the assets to be distributed.**

   An *estate planner* can help develop your goals based on experience with other estates. Usually the estate planner is an attorney who specializes in this area. When a valuable or complicated estate is involved, a team of financial professionals may work on the plan, including a financial planner, an accountant, an insurance agent or broker, and a financial planner or other investment professional. Usually one professional is the leader or "quarterback" in charge of the big picture and coordination while the others concentrate on specific areas.

4. **Consider secondary goals.**

   Examples of secondary goals include placing controls or restrictions on inheritances instead of giving property directly. An estate plan often involves trade-offs, because fully reaching all your goals may not be possible. You may have to decide that some goals are more important than others.

5. **Resolve how much property to give now and how much to give later.**

   You can reap both tax and nontax benefits if you make lifetime gifts instead of waiting to make bequests through your estate. I discuss these benefits and other aspects of lifetime giving throughout the "Decreasing Your Estate Taxes" section.

6. **Work with one or more estate planning professionals to develop your estate plan.**

   After you assess your assets and liabilities, cash flow, and goals, it's time to work with one or more professionals to develop a plan. A typical middle-class family usually needs to work only with an estate planning attorney or an attorney and a financial planner or accountant. Wealthier individuals, especially those who own businesses or other complicated assets, may need a team that includes one or more attorneys, an accountant, a life insurance broker, a business appraiser, a trustee, and other professionals.

7. **Understand your estate plan.**

   Be an active participant in developing your plan and be sure you understand it. Don't be afraid to ask questions if you don't understand something.

8. Implement the plan.

You had an estate plan created for good reasons, and you spent lots of time and money on it. So, be sure to implement it; otherwise, your estate may be in jeopardy later. Your will, trusts, and any other documents need to be legally executed (signed and witnessed or notarized as required by your state's law). Legal ownership of assets needs to be transferred to trusts. If the plan is to make gifts to loved ones or charity, be sure the gifts are made as scheduled. After a plan is developed, your estate planner should provide a checklist of actions you need to take. Be sure to follow through and take those actions.

9. Explain the general idea of the plan to your heirs.

The top reason for estate disputes is probably surprise. When one or more heirs are surprised by the details of the estate plan, hurt feelings can lead to disputes. For example, if you have several children but don't plan to have your estate divided equally among them, you should discuss this individually with your adult children and explain your reasoning. You can reduce the potential for disputes by telling family members, in general, what the plan is, especially any terms that may surprise someone. Doing so gives your loved ones a chance to absorb the news, ask questions, and hear your explanation.

REMEMBER

Most estate planners don't recommend that you give family members (other than the persons picked to be executors or trustees) copies of the will or other estate planning documents. They don't need to see every detail in advance. Besides, you'll likely need to modify the plan every few years, resulting in the need to circulate copies after every change. Finally, you don't want multiple copies of your will circulating. When it comes time for the will to be probated, disputes could arise over which is the latest valid version.

10. Review and update the plan.

An estate plan isn't fixed and permanent — your situation evolves. The tax law, financial environment, and other factors change. Every two to three years or so, meet with your estate planner to review the plan, compare it to changes in your life and the law, and decide whether adjustments should be made. You also should meet with the estate planner after major changes in your family, such as births, deaths, marriages, and divorces.

Studying some strategies before starting your estate plan

Estate planning can be overwhelming at first. Attorneys use their own language, and many of them can't translate their jargon for regular folks. Some attorneys and estate planners also like to use a cookie-cutter approach, offering the same basic estate plan to almost everyone without explanation or consideration for the person's situation. Even when an attorney explains things well, the plan can be confusing because a wide range of strategies is available, and each has different advantages and disadvantages.

Despite some of the confusing messages you may receive, you should know some basic rules and guidelines that apply to every estate plan. That's because although strategies and tools differ between plans, some key principles apply whether an estate is worth $50,000 or $50 million. Study the principles in the following sections before meeting with an estate planner and diving into the details of will clauses, trusts, probate, and the like.

Finish your plan no matter what

Many people don't start or don't finish estate plans because they can't resolve certain issues. Estate plans can get stalled for any number of reasons. Don't let such issues leave you with no estate plan.

Some of these issues may include the following:

>> Spouses may not agree on who should be guardians of their children or whether to restrict the control adult children have over their inheritances.

>> An estate owner may be uncertain whether to give equally to the children or how much to give to charity.

>> In large or complicated estates, the owner may be unable to choose from among different strategies offered by the estate planner.

REMEMBER

You don't need to complete an estate plan in one step; creating it in phases is actually a smarter move. That's because some things can be changed easily while others are irreversible. For example, you may start with a basic will and powers of attorney. (These are discussed later in this chapter.) Over time, goals can be developed and refined, disagreements resolved, and the rest of the plan (such as trusts, gifts, and business succession plans) put in place.

Keep track of your estate

When putting together your estate plan, keep detailed records and maintain a complete list of your assets and liabilities (and the estate administrator and estate planner need to know where to locate that list). The list should include the following information:

>> Account names and numbers

>> Balances as of a certain date

>> Contact information

>> Internet passwords and usernames

REMEMBER

Your estate administrator may be able to locate all your assets in a reasonable time and be able to process your estate without a list of assets and liabilities. However, searching for the information drives up the expense and time involved in processing the estate, delaying the settlement and distribution. Also, the recommended estate plan may have been different if the overlooked assets had been known earlier.

TIP

To help your estate administrator and heirs, prepare a notebook that includes statements of your assets and liabilities and cash flow. Include copies of recent account statements, income tax returns, and other ownership information (or at least note where this information can be found). Update the notebook annually, and let your administrator know where it can be located.

Don't forget to include any "digital assets" or accounts in your list. The list should include details of how the accounts or assets can be accessed, such as passwords, usernames, and security questions. Otherwise, your executor and loved ones will have trouble accessing and taking necessary actions with these assets. Also, include details of any payments that are automatically deducted from a financial account or debited to a credit card.

WARNING

Here are some common pitfalls to avoid:

>> Estate owners may open a number of investment accounts over the years and then do little with them.

>> Balances may be left in the retirement plans of former employers.

>> Life insurance policies and annuities may be purchased and left in drawers or files.

Estimate cash flow

Estates need cash for all these reasons and more:

>> If you have dependents, their expenses must be paid while the estate is being processed.

>> The expenses of maintaining your estate, especially the costs of running your home and other properties, need to be paid.

>> The expenses of the estate, such as lawyer's fees, probate court costs, and taxes, need to be paid.

>> Your debts must be paid.

A number of estates, unfortunately, are asset rich and cash poor. The estate owners reduced taxes and decided how to divide their assets, but they didn't ensure that their estates had enough cash (or assets that could easily be converted to cash).

WARNING

Your estate can't be processed and distributed to heirs until all the debts and expenses are paid. If enough cash isn't available to make payments, assets must be sold. In this case, you risk having assets sold in a hurry and possibly at distress prices simply to raise cash. To avoid this unpleasant outcome, be sure cash flow planning is part of your estate plan.

Don't wait for the perfect plan

Estate planning involves trade-offs. Among the trade-offs are those relating to your goals, estate taxes, the needs and desires of your family, charitable inclinations, and the economy and financial markets. Don't expect an estate plan to be perfect, and don't expect there to be one right plan for you.

Except for simple, basic estates, estate planners present choices and alternatives. Each has advantages and disadvantages. As the estate owner, you decide the plan features that have the best trade-offs among the many factors.

Carefully choose executors and trustees

Make sure you take your time to select the right executors and trustees for your estate. Executors and trustees are the people who implement your estate plans. The *executor* (or *administrator*) is the person who manages the estate, shepherds it through probate court, and distributes the assets. A *trustee* controls any property that was put in a trust and manages it according to the trust agreement and state law.

The executor and trustee don't have to be the same person. In fact, it may be a good idea to name different people. A trustee, for example, is likely to manage property for much longer than an executor, and the responsibilities of the two jobs are different.

Often, the selection of executors and trustees is an afterthought. The executor usually is the oldest adult child of the estate owner; it also can be the estate planning lawyer. The trustee is a bank suggested by the lawyer. These may or may not be good choices; if better choices are evident for you, go with those. Too often good estate plans are ruined because the wrong people are selected for these jobs. These folks may not be suitable for the positions or may not understand what the estate owner wanted.

TIP

When deciding who your executor and trustee will be, consider personal skills, time commitment, cost, and knowledge of your family and your wishes. For some, the best compromise is to name both a family member and a lawyer or other professional to share the positions as co-executors or co-trustees. You can either divide their duties or require them to agree on each item before taking action.

REMEMBER

No matter who you decide on for these positions, make your choices known to family members. Early notice gives them an opportunity to get used to the decisions and gives you an idea of whether it will work.

Anticipate conflicts

Most estate problems occur because of conflicts. When planning your estate, consider the potential conflicts and structure the plan to avoid or minimize them.

You may encounter different types of conflicts, such as from the following:

>> **Family members:** They sometimes have personality conflicts. For example, maybe two or more members simply don't get along. You won't be around to mediate the disputes or keep people in line. With money at stake — and the death of a loved one charging relatives' emotions — don't expect these members to suddenly be able to manage property jointly or share the property. A better solution may be to give each of them sole ownership of different assets. If that means directing the executor to sell assets and distribute the cash, you probably should do that as long as you understand the consequences of doing so and are comfortable with those.

Or suppose your plan for dividing the personal property of the estate is to let the children decide among themselves. In some families this method works. In other families, the children argue over the process and ultimately how the assets are divided.

>> **The actual estate plan:** Suppose you put most of your estate in a trust and name your spouse trustee. That trust is intended to support your spouse for life, and the remainder of it goes to your children. The children may decide the trust should be invested more for long-term growth, while your spouse may invest it to maximize income. The situation could lead to hard feelings and perhaps litigation (even though your spouse is named trustee).

TIP

You know your family. Do your best to assess how the members may react to different parts of the plan, and change the plan if you foresee conflicts and disputes. Also, benefit from the guidance and input of a competent planning professional who has witnessed firsthand what works and what causes conflicts in similar family situations. You may be uncomfortable or embarrassed at the thought of discussing some family situations with a stranger, but your estate planner likely has seen or heard it all before.

Why everyone needs a will

A will is the most basic estate planning document, and for most people, particularly those who are younger or don't have great assets, the only critical one. Through a will, you can direct to whom your assets will go upon your death, as well as who will serve as guardian for your minor children.

In the absence of a will, state law dictates these important issues. Thus, your friends, less closely related relatives, and charities will likely receive nothing.

TIP

Also, make sure that your named beneficiaries on IRA accounts, for example, reflect your current wishes. Many people mistakenly believe that a will overrides their beneficiary statement or insurance.

Without a will, your heirs are powerless, and the state will appoint an administrator to supervise the distribution of your assets at a fee of around 5 percent of your estate. A bond must also be posted at a cost of hundreds of dollars.

In the event that both you and your spouse die without a will, the state (courts and social service agencies) will decide who will raise your children. Even if you can't decide at this time who you want to raise your children, you should at least appoint a trusted guardian who can decide for you.

If you previously completed a will, how many years ago was it prepared, and have any significant changes happened in your life since then (for example, a move, the birth of a child, the passing of a named beneficiary, and so on)? If so, consider updating your will.

REMEMBER

A will isn't set in stone. You can change it over time as needed, so don't avoid making a will just because you haven't decided certain issues. If you're not sure about a few details, have a basic will prepared now and then change it as needed in future years.

Avoiding probate through living trusts

Because of the United States' quirky legal system, even if you have a will, some or all of your assets must go through a court process known as probate. *Probate* is the legal process for administering and implementing the directions in a will. Property and assets that are owned in joint tenancy or inside retirement accounts, such as IRAs or 401(k)s, generally pass to heirs without having to go through probate. However, most other assets are probated.

A *living trust* effectively transfers assets into a trust. As the trustee, you control those assets, and you can revoke the trust whenever you desire. The advantage of a living trust is that upon your death, assets can pass directly to your beneficiaries without going through probate. Probate can be a lengthy, expensive hassle for your heirs — with legal fees tallying 5 percent or more of the value of the estate. In addition, your assets become a matter of public record as a result of probate.

Living trusts are likely to be of greatest value to people who meet one or more of the following criteria (the more that apply, the more value trusts have):

>> Age 60 or older

>> Single

>> Assets worth more than $100,000 that must pass through probate (including real estate, nonretirement accounts, and small businesses)

>> Real property held in other states

As with a will, you do *not* need an attorney to establish a legal and valid living trust. Attorney fees for establishing a living trust can range from hundreds to thousands of dollars. Hiring an attorney is of greatest value to people with large estates who don't have the time, desire, and expertise to maximize the value derived from estate planning. Also consult with an attorney if you have non-standard wishes to be carried out, such as special-needs beneficiaries or extra control measures you want applied to assets after incapacity or death.

Note: Living trusts keep assets out of probate but have nothing to do with minimizing estate or inheritance taxes.

Power of attorney: Appointing your financial sidekick

One of the most important documents in a good estate plan (other than a will, which I discuss in the preceding section) is the *financial power of attorney* (POA). This document designates someone (or several people) to take financial actions when you are unable. They can pay bills, change investments, and make other necessary moves. They even can make estate planning gifts if you provide that in the document.

REMEMBER

Unlike the will, the financial power of attorney takes effect while you're alive but unable to act because of a temporary or permanent disability.

The POA is a document I hope you don't ever need, but like insurance, you need to prepare it ahead of time to ensure you have it if you ever need to use it. Without the POA (or a living trust, which I discuss previously in this chapter), your finances can't be managed without your approval. Any property solely in your name, including your business, legally can't be sold or managed by anyone else. Bills can't be paid, and your portfolio can't be managed. Loans can't be taken out against your assets.

Answering Key Questions to Gather Critical Information

A major reason that people don't have estate plans is they don't know how to begin. Following are the key estate planning questions relating to who should receive the wealth, how much each recipient should receive, when the wealth should be transferred, and how the wealth should be transferred.

>> **Who's in charge?** Your estate needs at least one executor or administrator (depending on the term your state uses). Also, every trust you create needs at least one trustee. The right choices depend on your family and its dynamics. Check out the earlier section "Carefully choose executors and trustees" for help with this decision.

>> **How much should I give now?** An important decision you have to consider before developing your plan is whether you'll bestow gifts now. If you give away property now by making a lifetime gift, the current value isn't included in your estate. Future appreciation also is excluded. There are some good reasons to make lifetime gifts instead of waiting for loved ones to receive them through your estate. You may receive a tax incentive, for example, or find lifetime charitable gifts to be more satisfying.

»» Should I apply controls and incentives? Estate owners always have been concerned that gifts to their loved ones would be wasted or make the recipients lazy, spoiled, or worse. Starting in the 1990s, more people began acting on these concerns by creating trusts called *incentive trusts* that distribute money only under certain conditions, such as when the beneficiary reaches certain goals or behaves certain ways. Age and other milestones (such as attaining a certain academic degree) are common restrictions that incentive trusts are based on.

»» Should heirs get equal shares? Most parents leave each of their children equal shares of their estates, but you may need to ask yourself whether you have reasons to consider unequal shares in your plan. Perhaps an offspring is irresponsible, or one is more financially successful. Or perhaps an offspring isn't involved in a family business.

TIP

When deciding how much to leave each heir, don't forget any lifetime gifts and assistance you made to them. One child may have received more lifetime assistance than the others. The children aren't likely to forget that even though you may have. To ensure that inheritances really are equal, subtract significant lifetime gifts from inheritances. In fact, some wills state each heir's inheritance will be reduced by lifetime gifts. For this method to be effective, however, you must keep an updated list of the gifts you want subtracted.

»» Should I exclude someone? Most states won't let you completely disinherit a spouse, unless you have a premarital or post-marital agreement. But anyone else, even children, can be completely excluded from the will. Many families have at least one child who is estranged, is a substance abuser, or has other problems. When the child is well into adulthood and shows no sign of changing, you can consider disinheriting the child.

TIP

Rather than completely excluding someone from your will, you have a couple alternative options. You can leave the inheritance in a trust with restrictions or just leave less than a full share. Be sure to include a clause stating any beneficiary who unsuccessfully challenges the will forfeits whatever they were left in the will. The trick is determining the amount that's meaningful enough to deter a will challenge but that's not more than you want to give.

>> **How should my blended family be handled?** There's no right or wrong estate plan for blended families. Some people provide for only their spouse and biological children. Other people decide their adult children from a first marriage are already on their own and provided for, and then decide to leave most of their estate to children from the second marriage. Sometimes, the second spouse is secure financially and doesn't share in the estate.

>> **Should I leave only money?** Some of the biggest estate problems and headaches are caused by nonfinancial assets. For example, some assets, such as personal property, collections, and mementos, often trigger disputes among family members. More than one family member may want an asset and be willing to fight over it. Some valuable assets also have emotional value, such as your residence or vacation home. You need to develop a way to distribute these items without triggering a major conflict. You can handle it in a couple of ways. You may set up a lottery or other system that decides who inherits the items, or you can leave the decision to the executor or have family members agree on a distribution.

TIP

To avoid these problems, you may direct your estate executor to sell all the potential problem assets and distribute only cash to beneficiaries. Even though estate professionals have experienced many problem situations, you know your family better than the estate planner. Get the best advice you can and then decide whether selling the assets is better than trying to distribute them.

>> **Should my wealth stay in the family?** If you decide to leave part of your estate to a person or organization outside the family, your estate planner can help decide the best way to do so. It's important that you tell your loved ones about the decision and why you made it.

Decreasing Your Estate Taxes

Under current tax laws, an individual can pass $13.99 million to beneficiaries without having to pay federal estate taxes (married couples can pass $27.98 million).

Whether you should be concerned about possible estate taxes depends on several issues. How much of your assets you're going to use up during your life is the first and most important issue you need to consider. This amount depends on how much your assets grow over time, as well as how rapidly you spend money. During retirement, you'll (hopefully) be using at least some of your money.

I've seen too many affluent individuals, especially in their retirements, worry about estate taxes on their assets. Here are some actions you can take to reduce those taxes:

>> **Reduce the gross estate.** An asset isn't subject to the estate tax if it's never included in your gross estate. That's why lifetime gifts are an important part of most estate plans. But you must be careful to avoid paying gift taxes or inadvertently reducing your standard of living. You can give $19,000 annually to each of your beneficiaries, *tax-free.* Any appreciation on the value of the gift between the date of the gift and your date of death is also out of your estate and not subject to estate taxes.

In the past, wealthy people gave gifts and bequests directly to their grandchildren (or trusts for their benefits) in an attempt to avoid paying estate taxes. Uncle Sam reacted to these attempts with the *generation-skipping transfer tax* (GSTT) to tax gifts and bequests made directly to grandchildren (or later generations). Because the details of the GSTT are complicated, I suggest you not attempt to plan around the tax without the advice of a good estate planner.

>> **Increase the estate's deductions.** The deductions with real planning possibilities are the marital deduction and the charitable contribution deduction.

>> **Establish a bypass trust:** Although it's no longer generally necessary at the federal level, you may want to establish a *bypass trust* to effectively double the estate tax limit for your state. Upon the death of the first spouse, assets held in their name go into the bypass trust, effectively removing those assets from the remaining spouse's taxable estate. (Speak with an estate-planning attorney.)

>> **Buy life insurance.** A strategy for paying estate taxes without reducing the estate is to buy cash-value life

insurance (not the less costly term life insurance). Your loved ones inherit the assets in your estate while the life insurance benefits pay the taxes. This strategy is more often used when an estate consists of valuable assets you don't want heirs to have to sell, such as a family business or real estate. Other methods for reducing estate taxes are usually superior, because they don't require wasting money on life insurance.

TIP

The federal estate and gift tax has gone through numerous changes since 2001. To find out the latest on the estate tax, visit the websites at www.retirementwatch.com or www.erictyson.com.

Using trusts to reduce estate taxes

In this section, I review some specialized trusts and help you determine when to use them. Many of these trusts are established at least in part to reduce income or estate taxes or both.

REMEMBER

These trusts must meet strict and detailed tax code requirements to achieve the tax savings, so don't try to establish them without an estate planning attorney. For more detailed information about trusts, please see my book *Personal Finance After 50 For Dummies* (Wiley).

Charitable trusts

In your estate planning, you can use trusts to make charitable contributions while retaining some income or wealth for you or your loved ones. These trusts can be created during your lifetime or in your will. You have two options with charitable trusts:

>> **Charitable remainder trusts:** If you want to give money or assets to benefit a charity, retain some income for you or loved ones, avoid taxes on capital gains, or reduce your estate tax, a charitable remainder trust may be a good option for you. The *charitable remainder trust* (CRT) is best used for appreciated assets (those that have risen in value) with substantial capital gains.

>> **Charitable lead trusts:** Perhaps you want to pay income to a charity for a period of years, and then you want the trust to pay income and distributions to you and any other beneficiaries. If so, you may want to consider a charitable lead trust.

The *charitable lead trust* (CLT) is sort of the opposite of the CRT (see the preceding bullet). As with the CRT, you (or your estate) transfer property to the trust. Then the trust sells the property and invests in a diversified portfolio.

An important difference from the CRT is that the CLT isn't tax exempt, because the charity isn't the ultimate beneficiary. When property is sold at a gain and income is earned, the trust pays taxes on it. However, like the CRT, the transfer of property is considered a charitable contribution and creates a deduction.

Retained income trusts

You may want to take advantage of some estate planning benefits with trusts without completely giving away property. With these types of trusts, known as *retained interest or income trusts*, the grantor receives income from the trust or eventually has the trust remainder returned. The charitable trusts discussed in the previous section are considered retained interest trusts, but the following trusts don't involve charity:

>> **Qualified personal residence trusts:** A *qualified personal residence trust* (QPRT) is a special trust involving either the principal residence or a vacation home of the grantor. Here's how this type of trust works: The grantor transfers the house to a trust. The trust makes the grantor the income beneficiary, allowing the grantor to live in the home for a period of years. After that period, the home belongs to the remainder beneficiaries of the trust, who usually are the children of the grantor. Because of this last point, the QPRT generally is used for second homes instead of the primary residence.

The goal of the QPRT is to remove the house's value from the grantor's estate at a low tax cost. When the house is transferred to the trust, a gift is made to the children. The potentially taxable amount of that gift is the present value of the interest the children will receive. IRS tables using current interest rates determine the value of the gift. The longer the children wait to receive the home, the lower the value of the gift. In addition, future appreciation of the home isn't subject to gift or estate taxes.

WARNING

When the grantor dies during the income period, the estate tax effect is as though nothing had been done. The house is included in the estate, and the estate receives a credit for any gift taxes paid when the house was transferred to the trust. When the grantor outlives the income period, however, the house isn't included in the estate. So, for the QPRT to have any tax benefits, the grantor must outlive the income period of the trust.

REMEMBER

After the income period, the grantor has no legal rights in the home. When the grantor desires to live in or use the home, they have two options: They can rent the home from the children, or they can allow the grantor to live in it rent-free, making a gift of the annual rental value. For these reasons, the QPRT frequently is used only after other estate tax reduction strategies have been used and with a house other than the principal residence.

» **Grantor retained income and annuity trusts:** Retained income trusts that don't involve a home include the *grantor retained income trust* (GRIT) and the *grantor retained annuity trust* (GRAT). In each of these trusts, property is transferred to the trust, and then the trust pays income to the beneficiaries (usually the children of the grantor) for a period of years chosen by the grantor. After that, the property is returned to the grantor.

At first, this circular strategy seems to have no benefits. But nuances in the tax law make these trusts an effective way to transfer wealth to others at a low tax cost. IRS tables that use current government interest rates are used to value the gift made to beneficiaries. When the trust earns more than the government interest rates and transfers that income to the beneficiaries, the excess income is transferred free of estate and gift taxes.

TIP

Estate planners generally favor establishing these trusts for short periods of time, usually two to five years. Assets transferred to the trust should be those that are expected to earn income or capital gains exceeding the government interest rates.

WARNING

The estate tax law is likely to be changed to require these trusts to last at least ten years to have tax benefits. Your estate planner should know the current law, but be aware of the potential for change when formulating your estate plan.

Special needs trust (SNT)

You may have one or more family members with chronic illnesses or conditions that require extra expenses, special care, or lifelong attention. You may be the person with the illness or condition, or it may be your loved one, such as a child. The solution for either of these cases usually is a *special needs trust* (SNT).

This trust is drafted so it doesn't count as part of the beneficiary's income or assets under government programs such as Medicaid. An SNT can be set up with assets from several different sources, including the person's own assets or those of their parents or with the benefits of a life insurance policy. Any remainder in the trust could go to the other siblings or other heirs. A life insurance policy also could be used to provide for other heirs while leaving most of the estate to the SNT.

REMEMBER

With a special needs child, it's important to use an estate planner experienced with government programs so the will, trust, and any gifts don't make the child ineligible for Medicaid or other government programs.

Dynasty trusts

Instead of leaving wealth to the next generation and letting them use it or pass it on as they wish, you can set up a dynasty trust, which limits the distributions to each generation. A *dynasty trust* basically benefits several generations of a family. This type of trust that once was restricted to the very wealthy is now being used more often.

In the typical dynasty trust, the parents set up an irrevocable trust (meaning they lose control over those assets and cannot make changes to the trust without court and/or beneficiary approval). Some parents transfer a range of assets to the trust during their lives or through their wills. Most often, however, the only asset is life insurance. When life insurance is the main asset, the parents transfer cash to the trust annually, and the trustee uses the cash to pay the insurance premiums.

TIP

The cheapest life insurance for a married couple is a joint and last survivor, or survivorship, policy that pays benefits only after each of the spouses has passed on.

The policy benefits eventually are paid to the trust. The trustee invests and manages the money and also uses it to benefit the family members designated in the trust agreement. The distribution rates and formulas are limited only by your imagination and goals. For the trust to really be a dynasty trust, however, the distributions should be less than the fund earns. Often family members begin receiving distributions only after reaching a certain age, and family members share in receiving a fixed percentage of the trust's value each year. The trust also may make loans to family members to buy homes, start businesses, attend college, or for other needs.

REMEMBER

A dynasty trust has more than tax benefits. The wealth is protected from creditors of family members as well as from mismanagement by family members, divorces, lawsuits, medical bills, and the like. Plus, assets in the trust aren't subject to probate as family members die.

A dynasty trust usually is limited to about six generations. At that point the trust winds down by distributing its assets to the latest generation or other designated beneficiaries.

Life insurance trusts

You may want to include life insurance as part of your estate plan. You can use it to pay taxes, to ensure the estate has enough cash, or to increase the inheritances of loved ones. Permanent life insurance is used in these situations. You also may own term life insurance to cover specific expenses, such as the mortgage, child education, and income replacement.

Life insurance benefits are included in your gross estate when you have any *incidents of ownership* over the policy. This term means you can't be allowed to cash in the policy, change its beneficiary, or take any other actions the owner of the policy can take. To avoid having life insurance benefits reduced by estate taxes, the policy should be owned by an *irrevocable life insurance trust.* This type of trust has an independent trustee who's empowered, but not required, to buy insurance on the grantor's life with the trust as beneficiary. The trust agreement provides that any insurance benefits will be distributed to the grantor's estate to pay the taxes and other expenses. Any additional amounts will be paid to other beneficiaries designated by the grantor.

After the trust is created, you contribute money each year to pay insurance premiums, and the trustee pays the premiums. The trust needs a *Crummey* clause for the gifts to qualify for the annual gift tax exclusion. When these and other technical terms (generally limiting your ability to control or influence the trust) are met, the life insurance benefits are paid to the trust and not included in your gross estate. Your loved ones benefit from the full policy benefits instead of the after-tax amount.

You may achieve the same result without a trust. You could make annual gifts to your children and have them buy insurance on your life and pay the premiums. Of course, this setup has no legal requirement that they use the gifts to pay the premiums. Another alternative is to form a partnership to own the policy. The steps are similar to those for the trust. This strategy hasn't been used as long as the trust, so the rules aren't always as clear.

Giving charitable gifts

Leaving wealth to charity is a popular way to reduce or eliminate estate taxes. The estate tax encourages this type of giving with the unlimited charitable contribution deduction. The *charitable contribution deduction* is for gifts to charities that also qualify for charitable contribution deductions on the income tax return. You can make charitable gifts with any of the following, depending on your estate plan:

>> **Trust:** Certain types of trusts qualify for the deduction and benefit both your loved ones (or you) and charity. See the earlier section, "Charitable trusts."

>> **Charitable foundation:** You also can make charitable gifts by setting up a charitable foundation either now or through your will. If you decide to do so, check with an expert on creating and operating a foundation because they're complicated.

>> **Charitable gift annuity:** A *charitable gift annuity* is similar to a commercial annuity, except the promise to pay you lifetime income is made by a charity instead of a commercial insurer. A charitable contribution is deductible against either your income or estate taxes in the year the annuity is set up and the charitable annuity will pay less than a commercial annuity.

>> **IRAs and other retirement accounts:** You can name a charity as the beneficiary of an IRA or other retirement account. Your heirs may end up with more after-tax money if you make charitable bequests this way.

Chapter **10**

Ten Keys to Successful Fund Investing

When you select a fund, you can use a number of simple, common-sense criteria to greatly increase your chances of investment success. The criteria presented in the following sections have been proven to dramatically increase your fund investing returns. (Visit my website at www.erictyson.com to see the studies and discussion of various investing strategies.)

Minimizing Costs

The charges that you pay to buy or sell a fund, as well as the ongoing fund operating expenses, can have a big impact on your investments' rate of return. Because hundreds of choices are available for a particular type of fund (larger-company U.S. stock funds, for example), you have no reason to put up with inflated costs.

Seek to minimize or eliminate the following fees:

» **Load funds:** The first fee you need to minimize is the *sales load,* which is a commission paid to brokers and "financial planners" who work on commission and sell mutual funds. Commissions, or *loads,* historically ranged from 4.0 to 8.5 percent of the amount that you invest (but have been less common in recent decades). Sales loads are an additional and unnecessary cost that's deducted from your investment money. You can find plenty of outstanding *no-load* (commission-free) funds.

>> **Operating expenses:** All funds charge fees as long as you keep your money in the fund. A fund's operating expenses are essentially invisible to you because they're deducted from the fund's share price, but their impact on your returns is quite real. Studying the expenses of various money market funds and bond funds is critical; these funds buy securities that are so similar and so efficiently priced in the financial markets that most fund managers in a given type of money market or bond fund earn quite similar returns before expenses.

Evaluating Historic Performance

A fund's *performance,* or historic rate of return, is another factor to weigh when selecting a fund. As all funds are supposed to tell you, past performance is no guarantee of future results. An analysis of historic fund performance proves that some of yesterday's stars turn into tomorrow's skid-row bums.

Many former high-return funds achieved their results by taking on high risk. Funds that assume higher risk should produce higher rates of return. But high-risk funds usually decline in price faster during major market declines. Thus, in order for a fund to be considered a *best* fund, it must consistently deliver a favorable rate of return given the degree of risk it takes.

TIP

When assessing an individual fund, compare its performance and volatility over an extended period of time (at least five to ten years) to a relevant market index. For example, compare funds that focus on investing in large U.S. companies to the Standard & Poor's 500 Index. Compare funds that invest in U.S. stocks of all sizes to the CRSP U.S. Total Stock Market Index. Indexes also exist for bonds, foreign stock markets, and almost any other type of security you can imagine.

Sticking with Experience

A great deal of emphasis is placed on who manages a specific fund. Although the individual fund manager is important, a manager isn't an island unto themselves. The resources and capabilities of the parent company are also important. Managers come and go, but fund companies usually don't.

Different companies maintain different capabilities and levels of expertise with different types of funds. Vanguard, for example, is terrific at money market, bond, and conservative stock funds, thanks to its low operating expenses. They also pioneered ultra-low-cost index funds (see the next section). Fidelity has significant experience with investing in U.S. stocks and is known for its actively managed funds.

A fund company gains more or less experience than others not only from the direct management of certain fund types but also through hiring out. For example, some fund families contract with private money management firms that possess significant experience. In other cases, private money management firms with long histories in private money management, such as Dodge & Cox, offer mutual funds.

Considering Index Funds

Index funds are funds that are mostly managed by a computer. Unlike other funds, in which the portfolio manager and a team of analysts scour the market for the best securities, an index fund manager simply invests to match the makeup, and thus also the performance of an index (such as the Standard & Poor's 500 index of 500 large U.S. company stocks). Most exchange-traded funds are simply index funds that trade on a stock exchange.

Index funds deliver relatively good returns by keeping expenses low, staying invested, and not trying to jump around. Over ten years or more, index funds typically outperform about three-quarters of their peers! Most so-called actively managed funds can't overcome the handicap of high operating expenses that pull down their rates of return. Index funds can run with far lower operating expenses because significant ongoing research isn't needed to identify companies to invest in.

The average U.S. stock mutual fund, for example, has an operating expense ratio of 1.2 percent per year. (Some funds charge expenses as high as 2 percent or more per year.) That being the case, a U.S. stock index fund with an expense ratio of just 0.2 percent per year has an advantage of 1.0 percent per year over the average fund. A 1.0 percent difference may not seem like much, but in fact, it's a significant difference. Because stocks tend to return about 9 percent per year, you end up throwing away about 11 percent of your expected (pre-tax) stock fund returns with an "average fund" in terms of expenses (and an even greater portion of your post-tax returns).

With actively managed stock funds, a fund manager can make costly mistakes, such as not being invested when the market goes up or just being in the wrong stocks. An actively managed fund can easily underperform the overall market index that it's competing against.

Index funds make sense for a portion of your investments, especially when you invest in bonds and larger, more conservative stocks, where beating the market is difficult for portfolio managers. In addition to having lower operating expenses, which help boost your returns, index mutual funds and ETFs based upon an index are usually tax-friendlier when you invest outside retirement accounts. In their attempts to increase returns, fund managers of actively managed portfolios buy and sell securities more frequently. However, this trading increases a fund's taxable capital gains distributions and reduces a fund's after-tax return.

TIP

Vanguard is the largest and best fund provider of index funds and ETFs because it maintains the lowest annual operating fees in the business. Vanguard has all types of bond and stock (both U.S. and international) index funds.

Steering Clear of Leveraged and Inverse Exchange-Traded Funds

Since their introduction in 2006, leveraged and inverse exchange-traded funds have taken in tens of billions in assets. Here's the lowdown on these funds:

>> **Leveraged ETFs:** These funds claim to magnify the move of a particular index, such as the Standard & Poor's (S&P) 500 stock index, by double or even triple in some cases. So, a double-leveraged S&P 500 ETF is supposed to increase by 2 percent for a 1 percent increase in the S&P 500 index.

>> **Inverse ETFs:** These funds are supposed to move in the opposite direction of a given index. For example, an inverse S&P 500 ETF is supposed to increase by 1 percent for a 1 percent decrease in the S&P 500 index.

Leveraged and inverse ETFs aren't investments. They're gambling instruments for day traders. As an individual investor, if you happen to guess correctly before a short-term major market move, you may do well over a short period of time (longer than one day but no more than a few months). However, the odds are heavily stacked against you. You can reduce risk and hedge yourself through sensible diversification. If, for example, you don't want 80 percent of your portfolio exposed to stock market risk, invest a percentage you're comfortable with. Don't waste your time and money with leveraged and inverse ETFs.

Reading Prospectuses and Annual Reports

Fund companies produce information that can help you make decisions about fund investments. Every fund is required to issue a *prospectus*. This legal document is reviewed and audited by the SEC. The most valuable information — the fund's investment objectives, costs, performance history, and primary risks — is summarized in the first few pages of the prospectus. Make sure that you read this part. Skip the rest, which is comprised mostly of tedious legal details. Funds also produce what's called a *summary prospectus*, which is an abbreviated version of the full length (*statutory*) prospectus, and which hits the important highlights.

Funds also produce *annual reports* that discuss how the fund has been doing and provide details on the specific investments a fund holds. If, for example, you want to know which countries an international fund invests in, you can find this information in the fund's annual report.

Assessing Fund Manager and Fund Family Reputations

Much is made of who manages a specific mutual fund. As Peter Lynch, the retired and famous former manager of the Fidelity Magellan fund, said, "The financial press made us Wall Street types into celebrities, a notoriety that was largely undeserved. Stock stars were treated as rock stars. . . ."

REMEMBER

Although the individual fund manager is important, no fund manager is an island. The resources and capabilities of the parent company are equally important. Different companies have different capabilities and levels of expertise in relation to the different types of funds. When you're considering a particular fund — for example, the Barnum & Barney High-Flying Foreign Stock fund — examine the performance history and fees not only of that fund but also of similar foreign stock funds at the Barnum & Barney company. If Barnum's other foreign stock funds have done poorly, or Barnum & Barney offers no other such funds because it's focused on its circus business, those are strikes against its High-Flying fund.

Also, be aware that "star" fund managers tend to be associated with higher-expense funds to help pay their celebrity salaries. (And star managers tend to leave or get hired away after several years of stellar performance, so you may not be getting the manager who created that good past performance in the first place. Index and asset class funds that use a team approach avoid this issue.)

Rating Tax Friendliness

Investors often overlook tax implications when selecting funds for non-retirement accounts. Numerous funds effectively reduce their shareholders' returns because of their tendency to produce more taxable distributions — that is, capital gains (especially short-term gains, which are taxed at the highest federal income tax rate) and dividends.

Fund capital-gains distributions have an impact on an investor's after-tax rate of return. All fund managers buy and sell stocks over the course of a year. Whenever a fund manager sells securities, any gain or loss from those securities must be distributed to fund shareholders. Securities sold at a loss can offset securities sold at a profit. When a fund manager has a tendency to cash in more winners than losers, investors in the fund receive taxable gains. So, even though some funds can lay claim to producing higher total returns, *after* you factor in taxes, they actually may not produce higher total returns.

Choosing funds that minimize capital-gains distributions helps you defer taxes on your profits. By allowing your capital to continue compounding as it would in a retirement account, you receive a higher total return. When you're a long-term investor, you benefit most from choosing funds that minimize capital-gains distributions. The more years that appreciation can compound without being taxed, the greater the value to you as the investor.

TIP

If you're purchasing shares in funds outside tax-sheltered retirement accounts, consider the time of year when making your purchases. December is the most common month in which funds make capital-gains distributions. When making purchases late in the year, ask whether the fund may make a significant capital-gains distribution. Consider delaying purchases in such funds until after the distribution date.

Determining Your Needs and Goals

Selecting the best funds for you requires an understanding of your investment goals and risk tolerance. What may be a good fund for your next-door neighbor may not necessarily be a good fund for you. You have a unique financial profile.

REMEMBER

Understanding yourself is a good part of the battle. But don't shortchange yourself by not being educated about the investment you're considering. If you don't understand what you're investing in and how much risk you're taking, stay out of the game.

Tuning Out the Noise

There are so many details, news events, and worries. Wars, inflation, deflation, companies laying off employees, politicians scaring us about something new or something old.

A key to being a successful investor is keeping your plans and needs in mind and tuning out the noise and minutiae. There always has been and always will be worries and concerns. Focus on what you can control and develop and stick to a sound plan!

Index

A

abundance,
  focusing on, 5–11
accumulating money,
  7–8
activities, importance of, 11
addictions, 30
Affordable Care Act
  (Obamacare),
  123–124
age of retirement, 143
aggressive portfolio,
  154, 155–157
Alcoholics Anonymous, 30
allocating money, with
  employer-selected
  options, 149–153
allowable deductions,
  113
American Opportunity tax
  credit, 120–121
annual reports, 185
annuities, 147–148
appliances, maintaining, 22
appreciation, 53
asset allocation,
  53–55, 143, 153
asset protection,
  taxes and, 122
associated services, as
  a factor in money-
  market funds, 46
audits, for tax
  professionals, 131
auto registration fees, 119
avoiding
  bad debt, 11–12
  "more money, More stuff"
    trap, 20–31
  probate, 168–169
  scarcity mindset, 6–7

B

bad debt, 11–12
balance
  maintaining, 136–137
  spending and saving, 7–10
balanced funds, 50
balanced mutual
  funds, 151–152
bear market, 65
board of directors, of public
  REITs, 110
bond funds, 39–40,
  46–48, 124
bond mutual funds, 150
bonds
  calling early, 41
  individual, 39–42
  obtaining prices, 40
  risks of, 58–59
  Treasury, 40
bootstrapping, 84
brokers, conflicts of
  interest with, 71
budgeting, importance of,
  31–32
bull market, 65
buying
  existing small businesses,
    85–88
  gifts, 9, 29
  on margin, 112
  real estate, 117
  stocks, 63–73
  technology, 27
bypass trust, 173

C

calculating total cost, 14
calling bonds early, 41

capital gains, 123
capital gains
  distributions, 53
capital requirements, with
  real estate, 106
capitalization, 48
cars
  fuel-efficient, 22
  reducing expenses
    for, 25–26
cash flow, 99, 165
cash flow statement, 160
cell towers, 109
chance, as a reason
  not to own small
  businesses, 78
change, as a reason
  not to own small
  businesses, 78
charge cards, replacing
  credit cards with, 14
charitable contribution
  deduction, 179
charitable contributions,
  29, 118–119
charitable foundation, 179
charitable gift annuity,
  179
charitable gifts, 179
charitable lead trusts
  (CLTs), 174–175
charitable remainder trusts
  (CRTs), 174
charitable trusts, 174–175
clothing expenses,
  reducing, 27–28
CNET, 27
college education
  financial aid system, 128
  homeownership and, 90
  tax deductions for, 120

About the Authors

Eric Tyson, MBA, has been a personal financial writer, lecturer, and counselor for the past 25+ years. As his own boss, Eric has worked with and taught people from a myriad of income levels and backgrounds, so he knows the financial and wealth building concerns and questions of real folks just like you.

After toiling away for too many years as a management consultant to behemoth financial-service firms, Eric decided to take his knowledge of the industry and commit himself to making personal financial management accessible to everyone. Despite being handicapped by a joint BS in Economics and Biology from Yale and an MBA from Stanford, Eric remains a master at "keeping it simple."

An accomplished freelance personal-finance writer, Eric is the author or co-author of numerous other *For Dummies* national bestsellers on personal finance, investing, for seniors, and home buying and is a syndicated columnist. His *Personal Finance For Dummies* won the Benjamin Franklin Award for Best Business Book.

Eric's work has been critically acclaimed in hundreds of publications and programs, including *Newsweek, The Los Angeles Times, The Chicago Tribune, Kiplinger's Personal Finance Magazine, The Wall Street Journal, Bottom Line Personal,* as well as NBC's Today show, ABC, CNBC, PBS's Nightly Business Report, CNN, FOX-TV, CBS national radio, Bloomberg Business Radio, and Business Radio Network. His website is www.erictyson.com.

Bob Carlson is editor of the monthly newsletter and website, *Retirement Watch.* Bob also is chairman of the board of trustees of the Fairfax County Employees' Retirement System, which has over $4 billion in assets. He has served on the board since 1992. He was a member of the board of trustees of the Virginia Retirement System, which oversaw $42 billion in assets from 2001 to 2005.

His latest book is *Where's My Money: Secrets to Getting the Most Out of Your Social Security* (Regnery). His prior books include *Invest Like a Fox . . . Not Like a Hedgehog* and *The New Rules of Retirement,* both published by Wiley. He has written numerous other books and reports, including *Tax Wise Money Strategies* and *Retirement Tax Guide.* He also has been interviewed by or quoted in numerous publications, including the *Wall Street Journal, Reader's Digest,*

Barron's, AARP Bulletin, Money magazine, *Worth* magazine, *Kiplinger's Personal Finance* magazine, the *Washington Post,* and many others. He has appeared on national television and on a number of radio programs. He is past editor of *Tax Wise Money.* The *Washington Post* calls Bob's advice "smart . . . savvy . . . sensible . . . valuable and imaginative."

Bob has been a guest on many local and nationally syndicated radio shows.

Bob received his JD and an MS (in accounting) from the University of Virginia, received his BS (in financial management) from Clemson University, and passed the CPA exam. He also is an instrument-rated private pilot.

Robert S. Griswold is a successful real estate investor and active, hands-on property manager with a large portfolio of residential and commercial rental properties who uses print and broadcast journalism to bring his many years of experience to his readers, listeners, and viewers.

He is the co-author with Eric of the national best-sellers *Real Estate Investing For Dummies,* and he is the author of *Mortgage Management for Dummies, Property Management For Dummies,* and *Property Management Kit for Dummies,* and co-author of the *Landlord's Legal Kit For Dummies.* He has been the real estate expert for NBC San Diego, with a regular on-air live-caller segment since 1995. Robert was the host of a live weekly radio talk show, "Real Estate Today!," for nearly 15 years, and was also the columnist for the syndicated "Rental Roundtable" and "Rental Forum" columns. These columns have been published in 50+ major newspapers throughout the country, and Robert has been recognized twice as the No. 1 real estate broadcast journalist in the nation by the National Association of Real Estate Editors.

Robert's educational background includes having earned three degrees all from the Marshall School of Business at the University of Southern California. His bachelor's degree is in Finance and Business Economics and Real Estate Finance.

He also has a Master of Business Administration in International Finance as well as Real Estate and Urban Land Economics, plus he earned an MSBA (second Master's) in Real Estate Development. His real estate investing and managing professional designations include the CRE® (Counselor of Real Estate), the CPM® (Certified Property Manager), ARM® (Accredited Residential Manager), the RPA® (Real Property Administrator), the ACoM® (Accredited Commercial Manager), the CCIM® (Certified Commercial Investment Member), the GRI® (Graduate, Realtor Institute®), the PCAM® (Professional Community Association Manager), and CCAM® (Certified Community Association Manager).

Robert has been retained on more than 4,000 legal matters as an expert in the standard of care and custom and practice for all aspects of real estate ownership, management, maintenance, and operations in both state and federal cases throughout the country. He is the president of Griswold Real Estate Management, Inc., managing residential, commercial, retail, and industrial properties throughout Southern California and Nevada.

Margaret Atkins Munro, EA (who answers to Peggy) is a tax advisor, writer, and lecturer with more than 40 years experience in various areas of taxation and finance with a mission in life to make taxes understandable. Her practice is concentrated in the areas of family tax, small business, trusts, estates, and charitable foundations.

She is a graduate of The Johns Hopkins University and has also attended University College Cork (Ireland) and the Pontifical Institute of Mediaeval Studies in Toronto, and she feels that her ability to decipher the language in the Internal Revenue Code derives completely from her familiarity with a variety of obscure medieval languages.

Peggy is the author of *529 & Other College Savings Plans For Dummies*, and co-author of *Estate & Trust Administration For Dummies*. Since her move to Costa Rica, she has become more fluent in cross-border issues facing U.S. expatriates living all over the world. She speaks on a variety of tax-related topics and has given numerous interviews to the national and international print and radio media relating her expertise in tax issues, especially with regard to their effects on families. You can reach her through her website at www.taxpanacea.com.

Jim Schell has not always been a grizzled veteran of the small-business wars, contrary to what some people may think. Raised in Des Moines, Iowa, and earning a BA in Economics at the University of Colorado, Jim served in the U.S. Air Force in Klamath

Falls, Oregon. Jim's entrepreneurial genes eventually surfaced when he and three Minneapolis friends started The Kings Court, at the time the nation's first racquetball club. Two years later, Jim bought General Sports, Inc., a struggling sporting-goods retailer and wholesaler. After another two years, he started National Screenprint, and, finally, he partnered with an ex-employee in Fitness and Weight Training Corp. Each of the start-ups was bootstrapped, and each was privately held. For a period of exhausting years, Jim involved himself in the management of all four businesses at the same time. His third business, National Screenprint, ultimately grew to $25 million in sales and 200 employees.

Relocating to San Diego, Jim began a long-simmering writing career, authoring four books (*The Brass Tacks Entrepreneur, Small Business Management Guide, The Small Business Answer Book,* and *Understanding Your Financial Statements*) and numerous columns for business and trade magazines.

Publisher's Acknowledgments

Executive Editor: Steve Hayes

Compilation Editor: Colleen Diamond

Project Editor: Colleen Diamond

Copy Editor: Christine Pingleton

Production Editor: Saikarthick Kumarasamy

Cover Design and Image: Wiley